STUMP RANCH CHRONICLES and other narratives

Rolf Knight

NEW STAR BOOKS
VANCOUVER, CANADA 1977

New Star Books
2504 York Avenue
Vancouver, B.C.
Canada V6K 1E3

CONTENTS

This book is dedicated to those generations of migrant camp workers, stump ranch philosophers, sometime union organizers and jacks-of-all trades who inhabited the backlands and the cities of Western Canada only yesterday. It is a tribute also to my father, who was one of them, and to so many of our friends during my youth. It is dedicated to them and to the hundreds of thousands of others like them whose lives and stories never were and now never will be recorded and told.

Unloaded freight scow near Grand Canyon, Upper Fraser, 1913.

Introduction

These chronicles narrate something of the lives of two men during seventy years spent on homesteads, in logging, mining and construction camps, on prairie farms and ranches, on stump ranches, in the west coast fishing industry and in cities of Western Canada. They talk about work and life on these and in a host of other jobs. They tell of neighbours, partners, hopes, defeats and differing responses to the conditions of the time. While their stories comprise a set of richly personal accounts, they also are a part of the social history of the homesteads, stump ranches and primary resource industries of Western Canada of that period. These accounts are not, however, 'merely' representative of a particular group or period. The extent to which Arnt Arntzen and Ebe Koeppen have retained their enthusiasms and vitality are somewhat unusual. Their narratives are filled with irony and humour, told with an inherent sense of drama, and are, I believe, as reliable as any.

The first account is of Arnt Arntzen who came to Canada in 1912 from northern Norway, already seasoned by experiences of primary resource work and related conditions. From scowing on the Fraser River during the construction of the C.N.R., through Saskatchewan ranching and Gulf coast trolling, his sixty years of work and life here span most of the modern history of Canada. The second account is of Ebe Koeppen who emmigrated from Germany to the Peace River in 1928 to enter into the last phase of the classic homestead frontier. The remarkable recency of these worlds may be surprising to some. The narratives are entitled *Stump Ranch*

Chronicles since they are somewhat distinct from the more usual homestead tales.

Homestead sagas frequently leave the impression that homesteaders were exclusively, and invariably remained, farmers. In fact, a general feature of most homestead areas was that many settlers were also engaged in primary resource industries and in other labour as wage workers. Most homestead accounts focus on those who remained to become 'the pioneers' of a particular locale. In the main they tell of those who 'succeeded' in remaining as farmers in their areas. There is often little indication that vast numbers of homesteaders—frequently the majority who started—sooner or later failed, quit or pulled up stakes and tried their luck elsewhere. The farming zones of Canada, especially at their margins, are littered with the mouldering remains of homesteads which were abandoned or were incorporated into increasingly larger farms.

It is strange that in the extensive literature of rural settlement in Western Canada so little has been written about stump ranching. The term originated as a quip about those blocks of logged-over timberland taken up by rural workers and aspirant farmers where the main crop was derisively said to be stumps. In B.C. the term had a much more general usage. In fact stump ranching involved a mix of subsistence farming, yielding some surpluses for sale, along with wage work in more or less distant jobs. Sometimes this wage work rotated with employment as small owner-operators in such activities as salvage logging. In many areas stump ranching was not just a transitional phase between homesteading and commercial farming but was an ongoing pattern that mixed rural living and resource wage work.

Two and three generations ago large numbers of men in the frontier areas of Western Canada combined lives as part-time farmers, as occasional owner-operators and as wage workers. These were activities which were then not so strategically different. Such lives involved an amalgam of experience which partly accounted for the evolution of wide spread, many-hued populist and socialist views in many rural and farm areas.

It is difficult to disentangle some of the sentiments which pervade so many narratives of homesteading in the New World. At times participants' accounts intertwine both vision and actual realities. Part of the reality was the hope for a new world with opportunities for starting lives anew, which was once prevalent among immigrant and native born alike. It is a vision in evidence at times in these pages, one which should not be dismissed or disdained.

Homesteaders and stump ranchers came from widely differing national and class backgrounds. Despite these differing backgrounds they soon found themselves adapting to the physical and social demands of the homestead world. They entered and gradually adopted many of the attitudes and habits current in those frontier areas during a period when that society still had the capacity and vitality to attract and remould men. They also helped shape that society.

Popular writers and the mass media have partly created and partly responded to an image of homesteaders as a hardy breed of rugged individualists alloyed with Horatio Algers. While such an image may have a certain ironic validity for some sections of the farming population, these do not and never did have an exclusive claim to the history and traditions of those who settled Western Canada.

Many strove to create cooperative movements and some even launched into communal experiments. Most were committed to the value of mutual aid, at least on a local level. Some canvassed and struggled to establish what were then radical and progressive political movements. Others contributed to the organization and support of labour unions during their many periods of wage work. In some regions they sustained a grass roots culture of reading, debate and critical thought. Even if the strength of rural populism and socialism is much reduced today, there is no reason why we should allow the Billy Sundays of free enterprise fundamentalism to defraud us of this inheritance.

The body of these narratives were tape recorded during the spring of 1972 and fall of 1974. They attempt to retain the vigour of the spoken record. Editing was mainly to provide greater chronological and thematic coherence and to incorporate elaborations made throughout the interviews. Questions and interjections by the interviewer have been deleted for the sake of readability. Deletions are primarily of material which was deemed repititious or similar to accounts remaining in the text. I have nowhere attempted to second guess or 'correct' the story.

The appendix of this book consists of a diary kept by Ebe Koeppen during his first five years as a homesteader in the Peace River country. It contains not only the usual items on weather and daily work activities but also records the wide swings of feelings, from jubiliation to despair, from joys and friendships to quarrels and complaints, many and sunderous. While fragmentary it provides a valuable and sobering counterpoint to the recollections of Peace River home-steading.

ARNT
ARNTZEN'S
STORY

Leaving Saskatchewan ranch, Arntzen family, 1941.

Ragna and Lloyd Arntzen, Bad Lake ranch, 1928.

From Another North

I'm beginning at the beginning. I was born in a little place called Rossnes, in Beier Fjord, about twenty miles south of Bode in northern Norway. My father ran a kind of trading post there; it was a centre for all the settlers in the fjord. Most of the people were farmers in the summertime and fishermen in the winter. Beginning right after Christmas they all took part in the great cod fisheries off the Lofoten Islands. Almost all the fishermen stopped in at my father's place to get their winter supplies, which they got on credit. The fisheries failed when I was nine years old. The fishermen couldn't pay and my father went bankrupt. So we had to move.

That was in ninety-nine (1899) and we decided to go up to Narvik. They were building the Offoten railway at the time, to get at the rich iron ore at Kiruna. That whole stretch was a sort of Norwegian Klondyke with people coming in to work there from all over the country, and from Sweden.

Narvik was quite a wild, wide open town then. The railway workers would come down the road to Narvik to spend their stakes. You know, those boom frontier towns weren't just here in Canada and the States. Of course it's different now—pretty quiet, but still beautiful.

We were very poor at the time. My father seemed to have a hard time to adjust himself. But my mother took hold quickly and she saw us through the first year by taking in boarders. Seeing as we were a big family my mother and father could hardly make ends meet. I had three brothers and four sisters. While we were in Rossnes it was fine but in Narvik it was pretty tough. We all had to go to work early. I had my first job when I was ten years old. Later on I got a job at the telegraph office and then as a mail carrier. Eventually my father got a horse and wagon and started a small dray business.

Anyway, I grew up in Narvik during those hard years. I had a lot of fun, too. When I was eleven I saw a troupe of acrobats giving a performance at one of the warehouses down at the dock. It impressed me so much that I put up a swinging bar between two birches behind our house and started practicing. After awhile I became quite a proficient acrobat myself and I'd have an audience out on the street watching me perform. I was a great lover of the outdoors and spent a lot of my spare time up in the mountains.

In the spring of 1907 I got a chance to go out seal hunting with an arctic skipper. I journied over to Tromso and lived on the vessel while it was being outfitted. In the early part of May we sailed from Norway bound for the Arctic. Now I had lived by the sea all my life but I can never forget my first day on the open ocean. To see just water and nothing else, no mountains or land or anything.

She was an English cutter, about eighty tons. A sailing vessel with a schooner rig on her. The skipper was one of the modern ones; he was one of the first to install an auxilliary gas engine. But it only run a few hours after we left Norway. Then it got stalled and we never got it going again. The propellor shaft had seized up because it hadn't gotten grease.

Well, we sailed straight north for Bernt Island, heading toward Svalbard (Spitzbergen). Eventually we hit the drift ice. We struck the seal herd right there and began hunting.

There were three hunting boats, four men to each boat. Two oarsmen, the steersman and the harpooneer. The boats were painted all white and the men had white jackets and white caps to blend with the ice. When we're within five hundred yards or so of the seals the two of us oarsmen lay in our oars and the steersman takes over.

Now, in hunting the seal the steersman faces the bow of the boat and pushes the oar instead of pulling. He keeps the oars right in the water so as not to make a splash. When we get to within thirty yards or so of the seals the harpooneer starts shooting. He tries to hit them right in the head. If he does, they just stiffen out. The rest of the seals don't take alarm from the shot because there's so much noise from the ice cracking and rubbing together. The don't even hear the shot. If the harpooneer is a good shot he can shoot fifteen, twenty seals before they take fright. But the first time he misses and the bullet scams into the water, or if the shot doesn't kill the seal right on the spot, the rest of them take fright and stampede into the sea.

We all get up on the ice and start skinning the seals and putting the skins into the boat. In the meantime the vessel has been standing by with only the cook on board. We row back to the vessel and stow away the skins. We get a bite to eat and then we go out after the seals again. At that time of year the sun is up almost around the clock and the only sleep you'd get for days was just short catnaps.

That went on for four, five days each place we struck the seal herd. In between there'd be a couple of days work separating the blubber from the skins and salting the skins and packing them in big casks. Then for weeks we'd just sail around and wouldn't do nothing but stand watch and eat and sleep.

I was a seaman as well, of course. We all took our tricks at the wheel. I never worked on sailing ships before but you learn fast. Young boys in Norway, always around those sailing vessels, it comes naturally. Almost like driving a car here—kids pick it up in no time. Besides, with the kind of set-up we had you didn't have to go up in the rigging too much. We handled most of it from the deck.

The worst was the bowsprit; taking in the foresail in a rough sea. You'd stand out on a rope with the vessel heaving up and down and it would duck you under sometimes. You'd really have to hang on. That water was cold, too. But I can't remember any particular hardships (laughs). Of course, when you're young like that—I was seventeen—you can take quite a bit without noticing it.

We sailed around the ice and took about two thousand seal. Then we set out into the Kara Sea. We tried to sail around the north of Novaya Zemlya but we got hemmed in by the ice. So we sailed back to the strait between Novaya

Zemlya and Siberia and sneaked through on a foggy day, which was illegal.

Once we were in the Kara Sea we stopped at a native settlement, a Samoyed village. The Czarist government used to send a trading vessel once a year with some supplies and they'd take out all the furs from those places. We weren't allowed to land on Russian territory without clearing customs and we certainly weren't supposed to do any trading. But the skipper thought he'd take a chance.

We anchored near this one settlement and rowed over to the beach. All the people came out and some of them invited us into their houses. They lived in some pretty miserable huts made from stones and drift timber. The people were very friendly but sort of child-like. They treated us to a cup of tea and were very eager to do some trading with us. The skipper done a land office business trading old rifles and rusty knives and axes for valuable furs—polar fox and marten.

After that we sailed quite a ways up the Siberian coast after walrus. In October, when we'd got our catch, we headed for home. Those arctic skippers were wonderful seamen when they could see something; they knew sailing. But when it came to navigation over long distances of open sea they didn't know too much. They knew the compass courses from Svalbard to any point in Norway. But they wasn't able to take observations at sea exactly enough to know where they were. So instead of heading straight to Norway we had to follow the ice pack over to Svalbard and from there we set a compass course to Norway.

The crew didn't make too much money. I only got about five hundred krone (approximately $150 U.S.) for the whole trip. I stayed home for awhile playing the flush seaman. Then I got a berth on a boat carrying ore from Narvik to Rotterdam.

The first few trips out of Narvik I was a coal passer. Those ships were all coal fired at that time. It was the coal passer's duty to bring the coal from the bunkers to where the stokers could reach it. When the bunkers are full you can just shovel it, throw it out to the stoker. As you work your way back into the bunker and it gets too far to throw, you load up a wheelbarrow to bring the coal up. When there's a rough sea it's quite a trick to wheel that barrow out to the deck without being tossed from one bulkhead to another. It was pretty tough firing too. We didn't have much ventilation and it got pretty hot down there. Many times, when they were cleaning fire—you know, when the stokers had to rake the clinkers out of the fire box—the coal passer would have to stand there with a hose and play water on the firemen. Otherwise they couldn't stand it.

In them days sailors was very fond of music because we didn't have any radio or gramaphone or anything. So anybody that could make some music was quite welcome. I had a guitar with me and I was a pretty good singer and had quite a repertoire of songs. I got out of doing some work that way. It was also my duty to go back to the galley to get the grub in big containers and dish it up to the crew in the fo'csle. After that I was supposed to wash up the dishes and stow them away. But I got out of that because they were so fond of music that they always offered to wash the dishes for me if I would play the guitar. Which I did (laughs).

I made a couple of trips on that ore ship and then I quit. I was ashore in Holland for about a month when I got a berth on a German boat, a small tramp freighter. I was able seaman by that time and we sailed the North Sea and the Baltic. We carried coal from England and brought back lumber from Riga and from some of the other Russian ports. On the last trip, we picked up a load of mining props from Archangel for Hamburg. I quit that ship there and took a train to Antwerp, where I got a berth on an English freighter bound for New Orleans. I thought I'd like to see a little of that part of the world.

In The Great Republic

When we got to New Orleans I found out that my ship was going back to England to lay up. I had been in England just before that and it was very hard times for seamen (1908). There were thousands of seamen on the beach trying to get a berth, without any luck. If I'd gone back to England I wouldn't have had hardly any pay either. I'd made only one trip and my advance would be taken out of that. So I decided to jump ship in New Orleans and try and get another berth there.

You could get shore leave alright, but the problem was to get my dunnage bag ashore past the watchman. Since I had no money I had to have a dunnage bag to get into a sailor's boarding house. If you had a dunnage bag to show that you was a seaman they'd keep you whether you had money or not. When you got a berth you'd get a month's advance pay and that's when the boarding house would get their money out of you.

Early the next morning I lowered my dunnage bag over the side of the ship and managed to sneak off the dock when the watchman went to sleep on a bale of cotton. I went up to a boarding house I had lined up the day before.

It's about five o'clock in the morning and I'm waiting for the boarding house to open when I see these two cops walking down the street. I didn't want them asking me any questions so I stashed the dunnage bag on the porch and walked away. After a few minutes I peeked around the corner of the street and the cops was gone, along with my dunnage bag. They had taken my bag to the police station. I didn't dare to go and claim it because they would have put me back on my ship again. Now I couldn't get into a boarding house.

Well, I walked around the streets and found an

16

employment agency. But they wanted fifty cents to register and I didn't have no money. I fell in with a young Frenchman there and I says to him, "I've got this watch. I wonder if I could get any money on it?" He says, "Ya, I think so. I know this place where you can get some money on it. Come on, but let me do the talking." I don't know now how I could have been so dumb, but I gave him the watch and he went into this pawnship. I waited for a couple of minutes but he didn't come out. So I go in and as soon as I'm inside I see that there are two doors leading to different streets. The pawnshop was on a corner. I asked the guy behind the counter if anybody had come in with a watch. He says, "Somebody came in and beat it right out the other door. Didn't stop for nothing." So I lost my watch.

I was getting pretty hungry. Not knowing what to do I went back to that employment agency. Just as that agency is getting ready to close this one guy comes along who had paid for a job in a hotel. The employment agent tells him how to get there—"You go up this street and down that alley and knock on the back door and ask for the steward named so and so." When I heard that I beat it to the hotel and got the job ahead of him.

The job was washing dishes in the Grunewald Hotel, one of the swankiest hotels in town. All the big shots would come there after the theatre and order fancy meals. They'd maybe only touch a little bit from one course and all the rest would go in the slop pail. There'd be whole sirloin steaks on silver platters coming back. Well, I was hungry enough that the first one didn't go into the slop pail. I was standing there with a steak in one hand and a wash cloth in the other (laughs). I worked in that hotel about three weeks. I'd accumulated seventeen dollars and I figured I was rich now. So I quit.

But the times were getting tough in New Orleans. It was getting late in the season and a lot of hoboes from the north were coming down to winter over. They were on the street looking for any kind of work. It was impossible to get a job. The only thing that was available were jobs milking cows in the dairies.

Well, I never milked a cow in my life but Christmas Eve

found me with just sixty cents left. So I thought I'd tackle one of those milking jobs. I paid fifty cents to an employment agency and had ten cents left for the streetcar fare to the City Dairy. They had barns with about a hundred cows out on the edge of town. I got there about four o'clock in the evening on Christmas Eve and the crew were getting ready to sit down to a big feast. I said to myself, "If they kick me out in the morning I'll have had my money's worth from this feed anyway."

The next morning I put on a brave front. I got out a stool and a milk pail and sat down beside a cow. But I sat down on the wrong side. The cow wasn't used to that and in about thirty seconds she had kicked me into the gutter. The foreman was there and told me to sit on the other side. "Oh ya, we used to milk them from this side in the old country," I told him.

That first cow happened to be a hard milker and I couldn't get much out of her. I was afraid to squeeze her tits too hard for fear she'd kick me again. So after awhile I said, "She's dry." One of the other guys sits down and milks a half a pail from her. The boss of the place went by and I hear him say to the foreman, "Christ, that boy never seen a cow in his life." So I didn't think I'd last there too long. But they put me on a few easy milkers and the fourth cow I managed to milk almost dry. The boss said, "Well I see you're learning. I guess you'll be alright in a few days." I worked there all winter but in the spring I quit and went up to see the fair in St. Louis. I'd heard about that fair even before I got to America, so I wanted to see it.

I got a job in St. Louis in a shop making railroad cars. After that I sailed on the Mississippi, on the river steamers, both sidewheelers and sternwheelers. I sailed up and down the Mississippi and the Illinois and the Ohio rivers for about a year. My job was what they called 'sailor man'. I looked after the ropes and the rigging and fittings and did some of the painting. We sailed down the Mississippi quite a ways, down to Cairo and below that.

During the winter we were laid up. So me and a partner of mine decided we were going to see the country around there a bit. We hopped a train and rode the rods down as far as Little Rock, Arkansas. It was pretty cold but we got into a box car what had a lot of straw in it; that had been used as packing for furniture. All the hoboes had found that car. There must have been thirty men in it, lying in the straw, sleeping. So we crawled in there too and laid down. After I'd been lying there about half an hour, half asleep, I feel hands trying to get into my pockets. One of those hoboes lying beside me trying to get my money.

Riding the rods was just the regular thing, just the same as thumbing a ride now-a-days. You found out where the trains would slow down and where you could swing on them. Or you could get on when they were stopped in the yards, sneak into a box car. As a rule you could give the brakeman fifty cents or something like that, if you had a little money. Then he'd look the other way and let you ride.

If you caught the train on the fly you might have to ride right on the bumper, between the cars, until the train stopped some place and you could crawl into a box car. I rode the coupling quite a few times. Strapped myself to the ladder so I wouldn't fall off. But I never actually rode the rods underneath the cars.

Coming back from Little Rock we got stranded in this lonely depot. Just a shed and a siding hemmed in by a sort of swamp. Me and my partner and two other fellows we met there. We were waiting for a freight. After awhile another guy came along and started talking to us. Then my partner, like a damn fool, called me over to have a drink. He had a mickey of whiskey with him. This other guy says, "By God, you know I'd sure like to have a drink. I'll give you ten cents if you let me have a drink." So my partner sold him a drink.

"So you're all on the bum? Riding the cars?", says this guy. "Ya, ya." Then he says, "Okay. Come on, line up. I'm a cop and I'm going to run you in." And he says to my partner, "It's going to go hard with you. Because you was selling whiskey and this is a dry state." He motioned like he had a gun in his pocket but I wasn't sure if he had one or not. Anyway, he started marching us away. The other two guys was pleading with him and I don't think that cop felt too sure

19

of himself out there at night with the four of us. So he says, "Oh well, I think I'll let you all go. I've been on the bum myself. Go on. You go back to the depot and catch the train." And he left.

Well, that seemed pretty funny to me. So me and my partner started up the tracks as fast as we could go till we came to stacks of firewood waiting to be shipped out. We crawled in and hid among that cordwood. About half an hour later we see these other two guys come hot footing it along and crawl in too. This cop had come back with about a half a dozen men to look for us. These two guys escaped just by luck. When a train came by in the morning we grabbed it on the fly and got out of there.

We were working on a bridge nearby when we found out how lucky we was. Some of the people working there told us about the racket they run in the prison farm in that county. You could get up to a year just for riding the freights. Then, while you were still in jail, they would charge you with something else. Like attempting to escape. Once you were in there they could do what they liked with you. There were guys picked up for vagrancy that been working in that prison farm for years. The county actually made money on that prison by hiring out gangs to work on some of the big farms around there.

Anyway, I went back to St. Louis and after working in the roundhouse for awhile I got sick. After I got out of the hospital I figured I'd like to work in the country some. So in the fall of 1911 I got a job with a farmer in Illinois. I worked in the woods with him that winter, lumbering. He had a brother who'd gone up to Alberta and had taken up a homestead there. He wrote letters telling how it was such a rich country that they could turn their horses out in the fall and they'd winter over on the prairies and come in fat in the spring. Well, that seemed hard to believe but those letters got me interested in Canada and I decided to come up to see what things was like here.

Where the Fraser River Flows

I got to Winnipeg in March of 1912, looked around, and wasn't too impressed with the place. So, in the early spring I shipped up to a railway construction job in British Columbia. They were building the Grand Trunk Railway and they'd gotten the steel as far as Jasper at the time. While I was still in Winnipeg I got to talking to two guys who'd been working up on that road and they gave me some good advice. They told me, "When you sign up, don't give them your right name. Give them a fictitious name. When you get to the end of steel don't go out with the bunch you came in with. Otherwise they'll stick you for sixty or seventy dollars transportation cost. That's supposed to be free, but they'll deduct it from your wages. Just go out on your own and then use your real name. They're hungry for men, they'll hire you at the first camp you come to."

So that's what we did, me and my partner. We signed on at Winnipeg and rode out on the train. When we got near the foothills I stood gazing at them for hours. Those were the first real mountains I'd seen since I left Norway.

Finally we arrived at Jasper, about two hundred men on the train, April 1912. A few bunkhouses was all there was, and they didn't have no blankets or heat or anything. It was cold too. So we all went back and sat in the train. After an hour the conductor came along and told us we had to get off because they were pulling out. "You can't dump us out here with no facilities," says one guy. "Well, we're going to," says the conductor. And they did (laughs).

In the morning a big fellow, a tough looking guy with a stetson hat on him and a six shooter strapped around his waist, comes along. He lines us up. He was going to march us up the line to a certain camp. My partner and me hung back, further and further, until we could duck down behind some bushes and get off the road. We laid down and had a sleep for a couple of hours. Then we hiked to the first camp and got a job there, no questions asked.

We were working on a rock cut right opposite Mount Robson. I worked there one month and in that time they had pushed the steel down to Mile 52. That was about ten miles below Tete Jaune Cache, at the head of the Fraser. They had a sawmill there and a crew of carpenters who were building scows. They'd load those scows with thirty, forty tons of freight and four men would float them down the river with the current. That's the way they took their supplies in. It was a cheap way of getting freight in to the camps. Just then they were setting up camps every three, four miles along the river so that there'd be thousands of men working on the grade all at once all the way down the line to Prince George.

After about a month of working on the rock cut with a pick and shovel I went down the river on one of those scows. We went down about a hundred miles and set up camp. I was making railroad ties there. Using an axe to cut 'dinky' ties for the construction locomotives. That was contract work and we got ten cents for those small ties. Ordinary wage work was three dollars a day and grub. A good axe man would get about four dollars a day but the ordinary pick and shovel work was three dollars for a ten hour day.

I got interested in the big wages I heard they were paying men to take those scows down the river. Five dollars a day and board. They'd pay you for the time it took you to go down the river and the time it took you to walk back. I had some experience with boats so I got a job as a scow man. After a couple of trips I got to be a captain. I got six dollars a day; that was big wages then.

Those scows had a sweep on each end, like a big oar, with two men on each one. You could swing the sweeps out over either side and row the scow just enough so that it would keep pointed down the current. Try and keep it away from rocks and in deep water. Some of the green crews made the mistake of keeping too close to the shore. Every so often one of them scows would hit what we called sweepers; big trees that fell into the river but were still anchored on the bank. A scow going too close to the shore wouldn't have no time to get away from the sweepers and quite a few men got brushed off and drowned that way.

You try to keep to the middle of the channel and row to give you some steerage. Of course most of the work was done by the current but you had to have steerage. You got to be expert in diagnosing which way the current was going to set you. By pointing the scow in certain directions you would eventually get to where you wanted. The reason was that the surface water would run faster than the water down below. The scow would be running in that deader water and if you kept the scow turned right that surface water would eventually push you where you wanted. When you see a rock ahead you have to decide which way you were going to try and dodge it. You had to start a long way ahead.

Scowing was a pretty dangerous business. The upper river wasn't too bad if you knew what you were doing. There was the Goat River rapids, but the worst danger there was that you'd hit a rock and hole the scow. That usually wasn't enough to sink them before you got to shore. But the Grand Canyon, that was a terrible stretch of water. Unless you knew your business there you were pretty nearly sure to smash up.

The canyon was crooked, something like an 'S'. You'd come down the first chute and the current would be running about twenty-five miles an hour. Then, all of a sudden, you headed straight for a rock wall. Unless you've got your scow turned sideways, turned across the current so that it would shoot out to the side, unless you did that, you would run right into that wall. Green men who didn't know that would smash up there all the time. And there was no chance of swimming. Once you were in that water you'd had it.

Then, in the Lower Canyon, there was a great big whirlpool. It would fill up, a hole ten or more feet deep and about forty or fifty feet across. It would suck a heavy scow in there and whirl it around like a cork. As soon as you hit that water you had to pull your sweeps in, otherwise they might knock you overboard. After about five minutes that whirlpool would boil over and throw the scow out and away you'd go down the river again. When the water was high that whirlpool got so big that it started to suck the scows down. So we had to quit scowing for three weeks. There were a lot of men drowned on that river. Of course, men were cheap. It was the freight that the company was worried about.

A lot of men moved from one camp to another and travelled down river on little rafts they made because they didn't want to walk. Even on the good stretches of the river there was a lot of things that could happen. Men would get swept off those haywire, little rafts, or they'd break up when they hit a rock or something. There must have been hundreds of men lost in that river while they were building the railway.

Anyway, I scowed for two seasons. We'd take the scow down to a camp, beach it. They'd unload the freight and break the scow up and use the timbers for something or other. We'd walk back to the end of steel, which took us five days, a week or longer. Depending on how far down river we went. We just stopped in any camp along the way for our meals and bed. The last scow I took down was going to a camp close to Fort George. But it was the end of the season and we got hemmed in by the ice ten miles above our destination. Seeing as I had a little money now and wasn't too anxious to do pick and shovel work over the winter I thought I'd look around a bit until the scowing season opened again.

There was nothing at Fort George but the Hudson Bay trading post and a few scattered houses. But in anticipation of this big boom that the railroad was supposed to bring some early birds had staked out a 'town' about three miles down river, at what was called South Fort George. One outfit had already built this big hotel there with a huge saloon stocked with liquor. There was nothing else there that fall, except a few shacks. But real estate promoters were staking out hundreds of town lots. Some of the promotional literature had more railroads and industry coming into Prince George than Chicago (chuckles). Even I bought a lot, which a couple of years later you couldn't sell for taxes.

It was the next season (1913) that things really got rolling

24

there. The railway building was at its peak and there was fair sized settlements growing up. Prince George was a wide open place. It was mainly a tent town with shacks scattered around. Some frame buildings on the main street. There were some stores, a few doctors, quite a number of saloons and lots of real estate salesmen. There was at least one big, fancy whorehouse. Some of them ladies carried their trade right out along the line. They'd come out to the end of steel and set up a dance hall there. Just a rough floor, not even with planed lumber, with a couple of big tents over it. There'd be a piano player and they'd sell whiskey and other drinks. Each of the girls would have their own little tent. It'd be three or five dollars or up to eight dollars to go and visit them there. And every few weeks when the main camp moved that dance hall set-up would pack up and move right along with them.

Prince George was really a tough place. There was a lot of graft and the local politicians and judges were in cahoots with the saloon keepers. When the railroad stiffs came in with their stakes they'd let them spend a good chunk of it in the saloons and then they'd arrest them for getting drunk, fine them for whatever they had left and give them so many hours to get out of town. The gambling houses were running wide open in town but if the railroad workers sat down to a poker game of their own the cops would come and raid them and haul them into court. They'd fine them thirty-five dollars and costs for gambling. Anything those guys had left over the thirty-five dollars was for court costs. That was the law as we saw it operating in them days.

Those railway camps housed men worse than you'd keep cattle. The bunkhouses were just five foot walls made with rough logs with a tarpaulin over them for a roof. There'd be maybe fifty men sleeping in them shanties. Doubledeck bunks made of whatever scrap lumber and poles was available. You had to pack your own blankets. In most of those camps they wouldn't even provide hay to make a mattress. Hay cost too much to ship in.

Them bunkhouses was crowded and smokey and smelly, and usually lousy too. There was no way to keep clean. They had a big heater in the middle of each bunkhouse and everybody would sit around that and chew tobacco and spit it on the floor. Dirt floors that turned into mud everytime it got wet.

One time we had an outbreak of typhoid fever in our camp. Some government authorities came over with a doctor to inspect the place. Well, they poked around a little and said that the cause of the typhoid was the impure water we was using. Here we had crystal clear water coming right off the mountain, and they blame it on the water. Nothing about the filthy condition of the camp. They blamed it on the water.

There's no doubt that the men working on the railroad was exploited to a fare-thee-well. So we are today, too. But capitalism hadn't moderated at all then. The I.W.W. came up and their walking delegates tried to organize the camps. I was a young fellow and joined it all right. Had a card and thought the I.W.W. was pretty good. At that time lots of the railway workers had kind of revolutionary ideas. When I was up there I thought that we were heading for a revolution too. But when I came out of there and began to see what other people were thinking I realized that there was no chance for a revolution. That we was only a small minority that felt that way. That didn't mean that you had to accept conditions as they were. But for years and years it seemed like the capitalists weren't going to give an inch.

By 1914 they were just finishing up building the Grand Trunk. But the P.G.E. (Pacific Great Eastern Railway) was starting to go full steam ahead. So a partner and me took a flat bottom boat and went down the Fraser as far as Soda Creek. That was quite an experience too. Soda Creek was a big centre for river traffic then, with sternwheelers coming in and supplies for the railroad stacked up there. The main depot for the supplies was Prince George because the Grand Trunk was completed by that time. The supplies and equipment for P.G.E. camps came down river by steamer or by mule team. For awhile we worked on the grade. Then me and my partner and two other guys took a contract to supply logs and timber for cribbing. But in August the war broke out and soon after they shut down all work on the P.G.E.

The first war took me by surprise. Maybe because I'd been out in the bush all that time. But I never figured that the labour movements in Europe would allow that to happen. But this nationalism seems to be a very ingrained habit. That war struck me as the most needless, senseless thing imaginable. It still does. There was quite a bit of anti-war feeling here in B.C. and on the prairies too. Most of them railway workers said they weren't going to fight in no war for anything. We didn't figure we had to be mixed up in that. And we were going to do what we could to stay out of it. Of course, there was a lot of patriotic types around too.

I always had a hankering to have a little farm of my own. So in between working on the railway I filed on a homestead ten miles west of Prince George, up the Nechako River. In between scowing seasons I went up there and did a little clearing. It looked like it was a pretty good piece of land;up on a bench, level like a prairie farm. No stones. It had been burned over by a forest fire years before. I built a little shack on it and I cleared about ten acres. The spring of 1914 I planted a crop. But then I found out the soil was no good, the substance had been burned out of it. We got rain and sun plenty. It was a good crop year. The wheat and oats came up and then got yellow and withered away. There was good land in that district but I didn't know enough about soil at that time to pick the right thing. But it was clear right away that you couldn't make a living off my piece of land. I did enough work on that homestead to prove up on it but I never really farmed it.

I went back to Prince George and got a job with a neighbour. He had a contract to take out logs for a sawmill there. We worked in the woods skidding out logs all winter. But in the spring there was no market for lumber. Everything went belly up. The sawmill went broke so he never got his money for the logs and we never got our wages. Finally we got twenty-five dollars each for that winter's work. In May I decided to get out of that country because there was just no way of making a living there. Everything was shut down, there were ten thousand men stranded in Prince George in the spring of 1915. One railway was built, the other one was shut down and the sawmills were closed up tight. So all the workers started pouring out of there. Prince George went completely flat.

Going out to Edmonton was quite a sensation for me. My partner and me took the train over the line we'd help build. We rode the three hundred miles that had taken us close to three weeks to walk sometimes and we covered that stretch in a few hours by train.

Saskatchewan, Saskatchewan

I worked in Edmonton for awhile and then we shipped out for the harvest in Saskatchewan. A bumper crop came in that year and I worked on those big steam threshing outfits, going from one region to another. After the harvest was over I wound up in a town called Fiske, Saskatchewan.

How I met up with Ole Olson was this way. I'd finished harvesting and was thinking about where to go next. Here I was, sitting in this cafe in Fiske playing my guitar and singing. This guy I'd never seen before comes in and asks me, "Well, where you headed?" "I don't know and I don't give a damn," I tells him. Well, he offered me a job as a hired hand at his place. That eventually led to me getting a ranch in Saskatchewan.

The next year I worked for another farmer near Saskatoon but in the fall of '17 conscription came in. I already had my Canadian citizen's papers and I had to report for the army. But when they gave me a medical exam they found I had a slight hernia. They gave me a class "E" classification and I wasn't called up.

I went back to Ole Olson's place. He had offered to go partners with me in cattle ranching. Olson had already taken up some open land and I took up a homestead near by. Our place was at Bad Lake, a big alkali lake nine miles north of Fiske. It only had water in it during the spring and we had trouble watering the stock until we located some springs and made cattle dugouts.

The first batch of cattle we raised turned out to be a complete bust. We bought a bunch of calves and raised them on prairie grass and hay. But by the time they were ready to sell the bottom had dropped out of the market and we barely got the price of the calves for them. Olson had been a logger before and he got fed up with cattle ranching on the prairies. In 1920 he asked me if I wanted to trade my homestead in B.C. for his share of the fencing and improvements we had made. There was about forty acres of good timber on that B.C. homestead of mine that he was going to log off. So we made that trade.

I managed to get a government grazing lease on four thousand acres of grassland near Bad Lake. I had a cattle ranch but no cattle. And no money to buy any. So I took in cattle from the farmers around there. I'd get three dollars a cow for pasturing and rounding up an animal over the summer.

Slowly I started accumulating some animals of my own and I broke up some of that lease land to grow feed. My own homestead was just scrub land, only suitable as a home site. All the good farming land around there had been taken up before I ever got in.

I put in hay for winter and later I grew wheat on a quarter section I rented. There were no end of things to do and worry about. Hail. Inside of a couple of minutes, it can destroy your whole crop. I lost many crops that way. We were in a hail belt there and every third year or so you could count on being hailed out.

Finally I had almost twenty miles of fences and that meant a lot of fence riding. My grazing lease was next to some rich, good wheat fields. I was always afraid that the cattle would break down the fence; they were pretty poor fences anyway. So I was afraid they'd break down the fences and get into the wheat fields and do a lot of damage. Do more damage than I could pay for. Even after I moved back to B.C. one of my nightmares was of the cattle getting into those wheatfields.

That was a never ending job, riding fences. Once a wire gets cut or broken the fence goes slack for half a mile and posts start coming down. As long as the wire is intact, tight, then even if the posts go over it don't matter much. But once you cut the wire, everything goes.

I had bached on the homestead in B.C. and I had bached on the ranch in Saskatchewan for eight years. I was thirty-six years old. I hadn't given up the idea of getting married but I didn't know how it would come up. I was always busy but I felt that there was something incomplete in my life.

In 1926, something happened that made quite a change in my life. My neighbour had gone down to Minnesota and his niece had come back to Fiske with him for a visit. Ragna comes from Norwegian parents but she was born and raised in Minnesota. For awhile she worked as a hired girl for some families around Fiske and we kept meeting. Well, I thought she was a good looking girl. But I thought she was really too young for me to be interested in. There was eighteen years difference between Ragna and me which at that time I thought was too great. But we kept on meeting and finally we fell in love.

Ragna had gotten a job about thirty miles south of where I lived. I could count on a sixty, eighty mile drive every time I'd take her to a dance. I'd have to drive thirty miles south, then drive over to the dance, then take her back home again. And after that I'd have to drive back to my place again. But I didn't mind that. I had a new T model truck and I kept her going all the time.

Well, I told her it was crazy, me courting a young girl like her. But I was so much in love that I figured that, "O.K. I'll be in heaven for a year or so then I'll be willing to be in hell for the rest of my life" (laughs). But it turned out well, very well. If we both live another year we'll have our golden wedding anniversary. And that's not too bad a record, even if it wasn't all smooth sailing all the time.

Well, we got married in 1926 and things looked just rosy for awhile. Over those years I had gradually built up and I'd got a pretty fair house built. I figured that in a few years I'd be well on my feet.

A year later Ragna was pregnant. We went into the doctor and he said, "Don't worry. It's not going to come in an hour. When she first feels it coming on just come into town." This was in the fall. Well, Ragna started to get labor pains and we set off for town. The pain got worse and worse so we stopped in at one of the neighbours. The neighbour's wife said, "You can't go to town now. We'll send for the doctor to come out." And Lloyd was born in our neighbour's house next morning.

How did I feel about being a father? Oh, it was great. That was a great feeling. You feel as if you've just grown up

But that also gave me one of the worst scares I ever had in my life. We were more isolated on that ranch than is usual for the prairies. Our nearest neighbour was about three miles away. When my wife was pregnant with our second child we had miscalculated the time she was due by about a month. I had been planning to take her to the hospital in good time. Well, on the twenty-ninth of February, 1932, we were sitting in the kitchen. There was a raging blizzard outside. My wife says, "Wouldn't it be a joke if you'd have to go and get the doctor tonight." "That certainly wouldn't be no joke," I says. It wasn't half an hour afterward that she started to get labor pains.

I didn't know what to do. I now know I shouldn't have left the house but I thought I'd be able to get help from the neighbours in time. Because a woman would know what to do better than me.

I set out across the prairie heading toward where our neighbour's house should be. You couldn't see nothing, but I steered by the wind. I was lucky and I hit their house. My neighbour and his wife hitched up a horse to the sleigh and I walked ahead leading the horse with a lantern held down to the ground. You couldn't see nothing of the road—all drifted in—but you could feel it with your feet.

When we got back to the house and I opened the kitchen door I see blood spattered all over the floor. I rushed into the bedroom, not knowing what I might find. And here is my wife lying with our new born daughter in her arms. She had a great big smile on her face and she said, "It's all right. And it's a girl, just what I wanted." Ever since that, whenever I have any fight with my wife, like married couples do, I just think back on how she looked there and I can't be mad at her anymore. She was brave as anything. Beverly was born just after I left.

By that time we were deep in the depression. When Lloyd was born, five years before, I figured I had a good chance to do well and really get ahead. But in '29 the depression set in and for ten years it was just hopeless to try and get anywhere. You could just hang on. And a lot of people lost everything.

I figured out one year, in 1931, all the foodstuff I'd produced. I had a fair crop of wheat, about three thousand bushels, and I had pastured almost four hundred head of cattle. Most of them belonged to neighbours but I'd pastured them over the summer on my grazing lease. All by my own work, without hiring any help.

I estimated that a pound of wheat and a pound of beef was the equivalent of any foodstuff. It would feed a person for a day. Just about anyway. Well, I figured out that with my own labour I'd grown enough foodstuff to feed five hundred people for a whole year. Yet I couldn't make enough out of that to buy myself a pair of pullover mitts in the fall. My wife had to sew up a pair of mitts out of binder canvas. The economy was so upside down.

We sold wheat for twenty cents a bushel and it cost us twelve cents a bushel to get it threshed. We sold steers for as low as a cent a pound, after you paid the shipping costs. Ten dollars for a thousand pound steer. What you pay for a roast now-a-days.

By 1934 it hardly paid to ship the cattle to Winnipeg because the transport costs were almost as much as what you got for your animals. So I slaughtered my own beef and started peddling it through the district. The very best steak cuts were fifteen cents a pound. Top roasts were ten cents a pound. Stew beef, what you'd buy cut as steak now-a-days, I'd sell for five cents a pound. I didn't make much but I still came out ahead of trying to ship the cattle out.

Most of the farmers were mortgaged to the hilt. What with the low prices and not being able to keep up on the mortgage payments many of them had lost their farms. The only reason that the mortgage companies hadn't taken the farms away from them was that they had nobody to sell them to. Nobody had cash to buy a farm. But as soon as things would pick up a bit, a little more money around, the mortgage companies were ready to sell them farms right out from under the feet of the farmers that thought they owned them.

So a big part of the socialist program was a kind of land

reform. The C.C.F. came out with the platform that the government would take over land mortgages and give the farmers a lifetime lease on their farms. They could will that lease to their children. Naturally the Liberals and Conservatives seized on that and said the C.C.F. was going to take the land away from the farmers. Of course it was no such thing. If you wanted to you could sign that lease and the government would pay off the mortgage.

I had to laugh. One of my neighbours, a young fellow, had bought a quarter section of land from a land company. He said he wasn't going to vote for the C.C.F. "No sir. They're going to take my land away." So I asked him, "How do you figure that? How much were you supposed to pay the company for this land?" Well, the price had been $2,500 for that quarter section. "And how much have you already paid on it?" He figured he'd paid something over fifteen hundred on it to date. "And how much do you owe on it now?" I asked him. Well, on account of the years he couldn't pay and the arrears and interest and everything, he now owed the company $3,400. He still owed them thirty-four hundred dollars and was getting deeper in debt every year (laughs). So I told him, "What you worrying about? You already lost your land. The C.C.F. is trying to save it for you."

In the thirties there was quite a few socialists, and some revolutionaries. Lots of them were what you call 'hard times socialists'. They could only understand it because we were pushed to the wall. And when times got a little bit better they changed their minds. The trouble during the thirties was that most people regarded the depression like it was a natural catastrophe, as something that couldn't be helped. They couldn't understand that those things didn't need to happen. That it was part of capitalist economics and was man-made. They kind of took it as an act of God.

Now I been of a socialist opinion even when I was in Norway. I read all I could on it, though the only time I been really active was there in Saskatchewan. I followed the Russian revolution all the way from the beginning and read the propaganda for it and the propaganda against it. For quite a few years during the thirties I read a publication called *Moscow News*. That was pro-communist.

You was so smothered in anti-communist propaganda, of the most stupid sort, that you couldn't get no idea of what was going on by reading the newspapers. For instance, the *Saturday Evening Post* had this one story about the result of collectivization in Russia that was supposed to be an eyewitness account. A story about collective farmers hauling grain. They were going along the side of a river bank, a whole string of tractors. The lead tractor went over the side of the bank and into the river through some accident. So, said this story, all the rest of the dozen tractors run into the river too because they figured they had to follow the leader (laughs). And that's the kind of stories you'd get in the newspapers.

Anyway, we worked hard on that ranch to make a living. I had twenty miles of fences to keep in repair and I'd be out there riding the fence with a hammer and staples, tacking up the wire where it had come down. In the winter we had to water and feed the cattle. That's a job all of us worked at, even the kids when they was old enough.

I guess my wife done just about every job there is to do on a farm. She cut hay and stacked it. She stooked oats and helped thresh it; herded cows and fixed the fences. She even drove the truck and shovelled wheat into graineries during harvest. And we had a lot of heartbreaks in the thirties. In '36 and '37 we had two dry years and I lost the cattle. Had to sell them; practically had to give them away because there wasn't no pasture left for them. In '38, seeing as I had no cattle, I ploughed up the land I'd used to raise feed and planted wheat. But it was a poor year for wheat and we hardly got the costs out of it.

Both the kids were going to school by that time. One of them little one-room schools that they had everywhere on the prairies in them days. But they learned well enough there, too. The school was four miles away from our place. In the wintertime that was quite a ways for the kids to go. If it was really bad I'd take them in the rig but usually they rode to school. When they got old enough to handle a horse and sleigh I fixed up a caboose for them, a sleigh with a little

35

house on to keep the wind out. If a blizzard came up, unexpected, all the kids from that school would stay with some family with a house nearby. They'd feed them and bed them all down somewheres and keep them there till they could get home safely. You could rely on that. That was one thing about prairie people. They were the most helpful, wonderful neighbours.

Lloyd, he's always been pretty musical. Both him and Bev were great singers. I used to play the guitar and both of them had good voices. Any social gathering going on for forty miles around wasn't complete without the Arntzen kids being there to sing.

We struggled along through those depression years. And we had good times, too. It wasn't all struggle. One thing we never lacked was food. We grew most of our own food and we lived well that way. If we could get enough for the winter coal we were all right as far as housing went. But to go into town to buy a pair of overalls or to buy anything was just about impossible. We just didn't buy anything. We couldn't buy anything. We had to make our own stuff, where we could, or do without it.

Our neighbours were wonderful people. We helped each other and lived a pretty good life together. We went to dances that they held in the school house or the community hall. In the winter we would have all night bridge parties with our neighbours. Or we would curl. Even in the worst of the depression we managed to make some pretty good times for ourselves. Only we couldn't see no future ahead. It wasn't the actual hardship we went through so much as the blankness of the future. You couldn't see no light at the end of the tunnel.

I had thoughts about leaving the ranch during the thirties. Sure. But not really seriously. Because it wouldn't have done any good. There was no way of leaving—and still being able to make a living. See, when you were on the farm you had no money but you had your house and we grew all the food we needed, except for a few things. If you could scrape up enough cash for the winter coal you were all right. It was hard to leave that for nothing. If we'd come out to the coast I might have been lucky just to get on relief. Staying on the farm was a lot better than that.

In '39 and '40 we had bumper crops of wheat and we got on our feet a bit. We could keep our heads above water. We were still only getting sixty cents a bushel. But in 1941 we had no crop to speak of at all. Seeing as I didn't have cattle there was no need to stay on the ranch in the winter. So I decided to go out to Vancouver to look for work. We all drove out in our old Chev truck. Coming through those mountains on that old road was something. Right away I liked it. All them mountains and the water running down in little creeks and rivers everywhere.

I got a job in the North Shore shipyards, scraping and painting ship hulls. Since I had experience as a sailor and was good at splicing ropes and cables, they put me in the rigging loft. I was in charge of signing out and repairing the gear they use for rigging the ship; blocks and tackle and slings. I worked in the shipyard and me and my wife liked the climate so well that we started thinking about moving out here. But we went back to Saskatchewan in the spring of '42 to put in the crop.

Next fall we came back out to Vancouver again and I worked in the shipyards as a rigger. We were getting to like the coast here very much but Lloyd was just starting high school and we couldn't move him back and forth. So we went back to Saskatchewan and I got into cattle again.

About a year or two later we elected the first C.C.F. government in Canada. They done a pretty good job, considering everything. You can thank Saskatchewan for the fight it took to put in Medicare. We wouldn't have had that here yet if it hadn't been for the C.C.F. And they didn't give away the natural resources like they did here in B.C. under the Social Credit government. That Social Credit is a farce anyway. They give away everything to the business interests for the price of some jobs. Well, they're just the backside of the Conservative party anyway.

Of course, the C.C.F. made their share of mistakes. The only businesses that the government seems to take over are those that have failed or aren't profitable from the start. The profitable businesses stick in the hands of the corporations but the government gets stuck with the bum companies. Look at what happened with the railroads. The C.P.R. got the lush districts and the government got stuck with the service lines, with the railroads that failed. The C.N.R. runs through empty country most of the way. It's the same with mining and other industries. When you have government competing with mining companies the government gets stuck with the poor mines that the private interests want to get rid of while the companies run the paying mines. To have any success in running a nationalized business you have to take over all the big businesses. And the C.C.F. and N.D.P. don't seem to be able to do that.

Sonja, our youngest daughter, was born in 1945, two days after the end of the war. In a hospital for a change (chuckles). Ragna always had the dread that the prairie was going to take one of our children from us. But it never did. She brought them all out here to B.C.

I thought about passing on the farm to Lloyd. Yes. That's what you always think. But it didn't work out that way. Lloyd enjoyed riding horseback and fixing fences but he was no farmer. We'd put him on the tractor and he'd do a certain amount of work and then he'd be back in the house. He'd always do what you laid out for him to do. But he didn't develop enough interest to do the various jobs on his own. I could see after a few years that it didn't suit him. And it would be silly to try and push somebody into work they don't like. He done much better for himself off the farm anyway.

In 1946 Lloyd finished high school. He was going to go to university in B.C. and Beverly was also going out to get a job. My wife and me would have been by ourselves on the farm. Ragna said, "It's now or never." So we packed up and came out to B.C. for good.

I advertised the ranch for sale and got quite a few enquiries so I thought it would be a cinch to sell the place. Then the price of cattle started to fall. I couldn't get a buyer. The next spring I hired somebody to put in the crop because I was working in the shipyards. There was a good crop coming in when, in the middle of the summer, it turned dry and we lost the whole thing. It didn't even pay the threshing costs. I had to sell the place for whatever I could get. Finally, I got a buyer for twenty-eight hundred dollars. For the whole place. Here I had a four thousand acre grazing lease, all fenced—twenty miles of fencing. The fences were worth that price alone. There was three hundred acres in cultivation. We had a good five room house, and a barn and outbuildings and all the improvements on our own 160 acres of land. All for twenty-eight hundred dollars. But that's the way it went. Anyway, I don't regret it. We got tired of the prairies and the cold winters. And I enjoy it here.

On the Coast

So here I was, in the fall of 1946, working in the Burrard Shipyards, over on the North Shore. By this time I had a job in the regular rigging gang. We'd refit ships that came in needing new cables and blocks and rigging and we'd hoist heavy machinery into ships that were being repaired. A lot of ships came in that needed new chains for their booms and new wire for their winches and such. So we replaced them. Although I was up in years I was fairly active. I could climb up into the masts and set on the blocks and everything. I wasn't afraid of that and I could do it as well as the next man.

I worked there till 1949. During those years there wasn't much shipbuilding but there were still ships being refitted. But finally work got so scarce and we had so many layoffs that I couldn't make a living at it anymore. So I decided to go fishing.

I had come out here with the intention of going fishing. That's something I always wanted to do. At first I didn't dare tackle it because I never had any experience with commercial fishing. But in 1949 I took our last savings and bought a small fishing boat for seven hundred and fifty dollars. I rigged her up as a troller and called her the *Sonja*. The engine was pretty shot and conked out soon after. I got an old car block, had it reconditioned and converted, and set into the boat.

How did I learn how to fish? Well, I'd been asking questions and watching other fishermen who looked like they knew what they were doing. Besides, I've always been fairly handy with gear so it didn't take me long to learn how to rig up and handle the lines. I started out fishing between Lion's Gate Bridge and Atkinson Point. The first day I got two salmon on the line. I got so excited that I pulled up all the lines and forgot to put them back down again (laughs).

I trolled for Springs early out of Vancouver. Later on, in May, I went up to Pender Harbour and fished for Springs there. Then in July I went up to Blackfish Sound, near Alert Bay, for the Pinks and Humpback and Cohoes. There were a couple hundred boats fishing up there at that time. It was the same story again. I had to learn how to fish there. We fished until the end of the season, in the later part of September.

That first year, if my wife hadn't taken a job I couldn't have continued. She took a job in Eaton's and we managed to pull through. I didn't make much money. Prices were poor. I caught enough fish the first year just to pay for my grub and my gas, that was about all. The whole first season I don't think I made over five hundred dollars. That's five hundred gross. After you take off the expenses there isn't very much left. So I started fishing for Rock Cod and I also learned how to troll for salmon in the winter. My catches increased year by year until I got to be a fairly good fisherman, for the outfit I had. One year, in fact, I was top boat of the day fishing out of Port Hardy. I got the biggest catch that day of any of the trollers.

I'd start out in the spring over in Nanaimo and fish out of Silva Bay, around Gabriola and the Gulf Islands. Then I'd go up to Lund, over to Bakers Pass, and get the Cohoe run there. Then maybe over to Campbell River for the Pinks and Cohoe. I'd generally wind up fishing in Blackfish Sound at the end of the season.

You soon learn to spend your time in the best spots. You learn not to waste your time and gas by patrolling around. Like up in Blackfish Sound—there was a regular trolling run. You go around Bold Point, past Bold Point Rock, and up Knight Inlet. It was just a run of about three-quarters of a mile and you go back and forth. That was really the hot spot of that whole sound. At first, whenever the fish stopped biting I'd move along somewhere else. That was the wrong thing to do. You just spend your time over the hot spot all day and eventually the fish come in and start biting again. They'd only be biting for an hour or so and if you missed that you'd lost your chance to catch fifty fish.

The most important thing in trolling, wherever you're

fishing, is to go the right speed and the right depth. And that's different in different places. You can't learn it out of a book. I'd watch the experienced fishermen and see where they spent their time. Some of them would tell you something and others wouldn't. You also learn to handle the gear fast when the fish are biting. When they're biting, the amount of fish that you can pull in depends on just how fast you can haul in and put down your lines. Another important thing is to have your flashers bent properly so they spin right. At another speed they won't fish at all.

I used to go to the Union meetings and I knew Homer Stevens. I always admired his dealings with people, a very able and sensible man. He never tried to railroad things through. He's got lots of patience; more than me. But the whole set up as it exists now is wrong for the fishing industry. I was in the union (U.F.A.W.U.) for quite a few years but eventually I left it. Most trollermen never joined.

To my notion, the best solution would be to have co-ops and force these canneries out of business. What I think is that seeing that we're paying for it all anyway, we might as well own all these canneries along the coast. Then everybody in the industry could get a share of the multi-million dollar profits they make. But fishermen is the most bull headed people in the world and they don't seem to be able to get together. I was a member of one Fishermen's Co-op that got started in the Gulf here. It was a good one, too. But it got in too deep over its head. When the canneries started offering a few cents a fish more, just to break up the Co-op, a lot of fishermen went and sold all their fish to their canneries. So the Co-op went broke.

While I enjoyed fishing it's pretty hard to do without your family. What I didn't like was that I'd be away from home almost half the year, more than half the year. I'd generally go out when the season opened in the middle of April and I wouldn't come back till the middle of September. I'd make a couple of trips home for a visit; just leave the boat tied up wherever I was and take a bus or plane to Vancouver. But when I was up the coast I'd be away for months at a time. I missed the family pretty bad sometimes.

We had a house in Burnaby, near Capitol Hill, and we liked the district. My wife didn't get too lonesome because she made a lot of friends here and used to go all over the place. Bowling, playing cards, and visiting. I think she's really come into her own since we moved to Vancouver. By that time Lloyd and Beverly were already married and had families of their own. There was only Sonja left at home, going to shcool.

Beverly, right after her first child, got T.B. and it looked pretty bad. She was in the hospital for seven months. But after she came out she had five more children and adopted one more. So I guess she came out pretty healthy. Now, after raising them, she's going to university to get a degree in political science. But I still argue with her about some things (chuckles).

Lloyd done quite a few things. He went to the University of B.C. to take engineering. But after a year he decided he wasn't cut out to be an engineer so he did teacher training at Normal School. He taught school for some years and then quit that and went to work. First as a floor layer and then as a bricklayer and eventually into carpenter work. He's a darn good carpenter too. For a while he had a radio program where he sang old-time songs, and he got together a Dixieland jazz band. But things changed and Lloyd went back into school teaching. By that time he had a fair sized family of his own. Well, that's not what you want to hear about. If you talk to my wife you can fill up a whole book about our kids. Ya, we're pretty proud of them.

We were getting on top of it. So I decided to take things a bit more easy. I wanted a small, fast boat that would let me run up into some of those remote inlets and come back without spending days and days in travelling. I got a twenty-four foot cabin cruiser that I rigged up to troll. But it was a mistake all the way around. Through technical faults, like not having the proper reduction, I never got the speed I expected. But I fished with that some years and made a good living at it.

Me and Ragna was ready to have a little fun. We went over to Norway in '62. It was the first time that I been back in over fifty years. Then we went again in 1966. That was a big reunion. All my brothers and sisters were there, we were all living then—my three brothers and four sisters. That was the first and last time we all been together since 1907. In the last few years we been dropping off pretty fast.

Norway was just as beautiful as ever. Narvik had settled down from its rough and ready days when I was a kid. It had all been destroyed during the war and completely rebuilt again. We went all over Norway and stayed with my relatives everywhere. Up north to the Finmarken (Lapland) and out to the West Coast and down to Oslo. We went back to Beier Fjord and sat up till three in the morning, when it was still bright as daylight. It had been quite a settlement of farmers and fishermen when I lived there. But now all those farms have gone back to bush. All the young people from them places leave to work in the towns. Like here.

A few years later, in '70, my wife and me took a tour through the Soviet Union. I learned a little Russian before we left. But we never needed it because there was always somebody who could speak English. We went from Leningrad to the Pacific. We visited Moscow and saw about a dozen places in Central Asia too—Samarkand, Tashkent, Lake Baikal.

On the whole I found things pretty much as I expected to find them. Some things wasn't what I thought, but on the whole I was impressed with what they accomplished. Considering they been invaded and had most of their country destroyed twice in less than fifty years, and had to start from scratch each time, they really done wonders. I was impressed by what they done with their cities. There weren't any real slums anywhere. Maybe you don't see the kind of luxury that you do here in Canada or the States but you also don't see any of the miserable conditions that some people have to live under here either.

My biggest disappointment—and that hasn't come from the trip to the Soviet Union—has been the conflict between China and the Soviet Union. I never thought that would be possible. I never figured that communism would produce saints but I always understood that the nature of that system would eliminate this kind of national competition. Because there shouldn't be the economic struggle involved. But it seems like the nationalist instinct is as strong under communism as anywhere.

Anyway, at the end of our trip through the Soviet Union we took a boat to Japan to visit the World Fair. Sonja was working as an interpreter in the Canadian Pavillion. Sonja's the real scholar in the family. She saw her own way through university with scholarships in Asian Studies. They introduced me as Captain Arntzen of the *Narvik*. And I didn't let on it was just a twenty-four foot troller (chuckles).

That year was also the last year I went skiing. Me and Ragna and Sonja went up to Seymour Mountain. I had Erik, my grandson, along. I rented some skiis and went up to get a ticket for the ski tow. The guy running it says, "You think you can make it up on that tow?" "Oh, I think so," says I. "Well, you try it and if you can make it the rides are on the house." I didn't have no trouble making it up on the ski tow (laughs) or going down the hill either. I was eighty and Erik was eight. We were the oldest and youngest on the slopes that day.

During those years we were taking these trips I'd still be fishing half of the year. Then the (Federal) government started to reduce the fishing fleet by taking fishing licenses out of circulation. Boats that caught below a certain average tonnage got a B license, which ran out after so many years. They couldn't be renewed, the license goes with the boat. There's still a few left, not many. Unless you could get an A license you were out. So if you want to get into fishing today you've got to buy a boat with an A license on it. Them A licenses cost three to four thousand dollars a ton. There was no such thing when I started or I'd never been able to get into fishing.

I still had the *Narvik* that I was fishing with. As long as I was in fair health I enjoyed fishing. Going out in the summertime. I suffered from the cold and wet but I didn't mind it too much. But now, after I got to be eighty-four years old, it got to be more effort than fun. So I sold the boat this spring and retired.

Arnt and Sonja Arntzen on the *Sonja*, Silva Bay, 1952.

EBE KOEPPEN'S STORY

Columbia Valley stump ranch, circa 1943.

Ebe Koeppen hand tramming, Stump Lake Mines, 1938.

Green Horns in a New Land

TOO SURE PROSPECTS

I would say that 1927 was not so much different than today for many young people who find themselves without work or without hope for a sound future. I was nineteen and I had no hope of ever being able to establish myself or do something I valued in Germany. I had left school at sixteen and my father had apprenticed me in a grain business. I was completely unsuited to and very unhappy in that crazy world.

Like many young people today, I had the romantic idea of having a piece of land of my own and of building up a solid future around that. Of course, I was completely ignorant of the demands farm work makes. For that matter, I was ignorant of any practical work. My own background was about as far away from homesteading as you could get. My dad was a lecturer on art and made his living, when I was a kid, by travelling around Germany giving lectures on painting and sculpture and cultural travelogues. He couldn't drive a nail in the wall to hang a picture.

Looking back, it was my great good fortune that I, in my ignorance, did go into farming. Because if I had known before what I had to find out by experience, I never would have had the guts to start. But through thick and thin, I always found farming very rewarding. I discovered that taking care of animals and working with growing things gave me great satisfaction. Even today that is one of the most essential requirements for anyone wanting to make a living as a farmer. The satisfaction that one gets out of making things grow is the main reward that one gets and keeps you at it.

When I was sixteen I was sent to Berlin and lived the

terrifying, lonely life of a shy young man in a big apartment house where no one knows anyone. Finding it very difficult to make friends or see any real content in my life. The apprenticeship that I was in soon proved unbearable. I was absolutely hopeless in business and office work. The great inflation, the insanity of living through that whole period in Europe when everything that you expected you could count on disappeared; that was part of it. That completely insane and hopeless situation created in me and many people a desire to strike out for something new and different.

Immediately, it wasn't the big political events that were going on that decided me to leave Germany. It was much more personal reasons. My contacts were limited and I was very lonely. I went to work in the morning and came home at night. My family stayed in the country after my father died. Sometimes I lived with relatives but they were always old people. At eighteen I fell very much in love, which had mainly to do with my loneliness, I guess. I had all these romantic ideas about "the knight in shining armour who provides for his loved one in every way" (laughs). It was a different world. But I lived in a sort of dream world anyway. The job I had didn't even support me, never mind a wife, let alone a wife who expected to live a middle class life of that time. It was totally unrealistic anyhow and when that romance fell through I felt I wanted to get completely away.

I'd been considering coming to Canada for a couple of years and I read about homesteading and where land was available. Most of that literature was so unrelated to reality, I soon found out, that it could be good satire.

I was thinking about all this and one day I see an enormous sign: "Come to Canada. Farm Workers Wanted." The C.P.R. had a big office on Under the Linden and the whole front window was plastered with this "Come to Canada" sign. And that's what did it for me. That's what made my decision.

I went in and they said, "Oh yes, there's lots of work over there in Canada. All you have to have is the fare and a hundred dollars landing money." For some reason you also had to come in under the Lutheran or the Catholic

Immigration Board. Maybe they guaranteed you. I don't remember now. It was just a formality anyway. I said, "I'm not a member of any church." "Well," says the C.P.R. "You better see a minister and join the church."

So I picked a name out of the phone book and called this minister. "I want to enter the church." "Oh," he says. "That's wonderful, wonderful. You come up to my home." When I went there he asks me why I want to enter the church. "Well, I want to go to Canada." "Oh," he says. "Have you been confirmed?" "No," I says. "Well, have you been baptised?" Yes, I'd been baptised. "Well, if you're going to Canada you can forget about the rest. That's alright. Just sign here." So I was a member of the church, the Lutheran church(laughs). They had that immigration business all organized.

Now I had to get my fare and the hundred dollars landing money. In Marks it was quite a bit and I didn't have any money. I didn't even have a job because I'd quit. But my relations helped me out, especially one uncle. They were glad to get rid of my for awhile. But they thought I'd never make it over here. I'd never worked with my hands in my life, never even had a job you could call a job. The kind of working experience and practical experience that most kids have nowadays, I never had. My farming was restricted to raising a few rabbits and helping around some of the farms near where my family went on vacation.

So my relatives said, "Here you are my boy. We'll buy you the ticket to go to Canada." And they gave me the hundred dollars for landing money. I'm sure they thought that in six months I'd be back again.

There was a friend of some distant relatives coming over to Canada too, a farmer about ten years older than me. Hans Boske. We decided to go together. We came over on a little boat, the *Westphalia*. I don't remember how long we were at sea but I was sea sick all the way over. There were enormous waves, something awful.

We landed in Halifax on March 28, 1928—Easter Sunday. Somebody from the Lutheran Immigration Board picked us up right there. He took us right through immigration—there was close to a hundred and fifty of us—and put us on a special immigrant train. The whole train was immigrants going out West. That was okay, that's where we wanted to go anyway, me and Hans, my partner. We got going through that Ontario north country and it was all burned over. "My God," I says. "What's this?" (chuckles).

FARM HANDS

When we came to Winnipeg a minister comes on the train and calls out a list of names and takes a big bunch of men off. "No, no. The rest of you boys stay on. We got places for you lined up in Alberta." Some more got taken off on other stops till we finally came to Calgary. They took the rest of us men off the train. "You and you and you. We've got jobs for you with farmer so and so." My bunch was supposed to go into town and report to another minister. The Lutheran Immigration Board got five dollars from the farmer for each guy they steered to him. These were big farmers and they needed lots of men. If the minister could send fifteen men, well that's, ah, seventy-five dollars commission. That sounded like pretty good money.

Me and Hans and nine other guys got sent to Mr. Schultz. He was an American and had nine sections of land in Rosebud, just east of Calgary. He was what you call a suitcase farmer. He only came up to farm in the springtime. He'd hire about fifteen extra men to put in his wheat and then he'd beat it down south again. He had about six tractors, if I remember right, and about thirty, forty, head of horses. A big outfit.

Schultz says to me, "You know anything about horses?" "Ja, a little." I'd been around trained riding horses a few times. "O.K., then you look after the horses." I was supposed to take care of the gear and harness the teams in the morning and saddle the riding horses and feed them and all that. The next morning I couldn't even get the harness on. The drivers come up in the morning for the teams and I've barely got one team ready, and they're all rigged up wrong. I had a hell of a time. One guy more or less did it for me.

The next day Schultz says, "You're not much good around here. We'll put you in the granary." It was very comical, looking back at it. Schultz would always speak in this mixture of half English and half German when he talked with me. He would say, "Geh zum grain mill und versucht die wire cutter zu finden." I'd look at him and run off in some direction and he'd say, "God, that man is stupid" (laughs).

We worked for Schultz putting in the crop all through spring. Then he set some of us to pull weeds, three or four of us. We were supposed to go out and pull stink weed, on nine sections of land, by hand. There was a law that he had to spend so much manpower rooting out stink weed. He would take us out on these enormous acreages, miles of it. He'd drop us off and say, "Go ahead and pull some weeds." It was about the most senseless thing you ever seen in your life. We could have pulled out all the stink weed on an acre or two. But there were thousands of acres. Absolutely insane. I worked faithfully for a while but then I did what the other guys did. Just layed down in the field and snored away. When quitting time came around we got up and went home.

It didn't rain a drop that summer. After a while the dust storms came up and started blowing something awful. They cut the young grain right out of the ground. We'd be sitting inside a solid house and the dust would drift right in. You'd clean the place up and in a couple of hours you could write in the dust on the table. By this time Schultz was back in California. The foreman wired down there and told him what was going on and Schultz sent a telegram back saying, "Let all the men go." So we were fired and we only had two, three month's wages. We only got about thirty or forty dollars a month anyway. It was June.

If you got to the prairies in spring there was maybe three months work. But that's all there was. Then there was nothing else until the harvest. If you got a run of twenty, twenty-five days stooking you done well. Harvest wages were fairly high for that time, six dollars, even seven dollars a day. But after that there was absolutely nothing. So at the end of September you had—let's say you'd got twenty days work—you had one hundred and forty dollars. Then you were on the prairie, winter coming on and no place to go and no work. You either had to leave or get a job as hired hand. How people doing that survived is a puzzle to me.

Hans and me decided we might just as well go up to the Peace River and look for homestead land. I even heard of the Peace River in Germany. That was like the promised land. When I look back on it I'm amazed at how accidental, how casually we made some of the major decisions of our lives. Very much trial and error. But that worked too. Sometimes I think it worked at least as well as the endless planning that's involved in everything you do nowadays.

FIVE EVENTFUL MONTHS

We had the name of this one minister in Edmonton who was active in getting people set up in the Peace River. We went to see him and he gave us the information about how to file on a homestead and so forth. He gave us directions on how to get to the Heart Valley. There were about eight or nine German settlers there already and he was one hundred percent for us going up. These churches all wanted to establish communities of their own nationalities and build up their own flocks. Frankly, I think it was a very poor way of settling the country. It didn't make for a good mix of people. And it didn't make for good citizenship because everybody was in their own tight group. There were large areas on the prairies where everybody was either Norwegian or Finn or German or Ukrainian, all isolated in their own areas. That's the way the ministers organized things. But luckily that's not the way it worked out in many homestead areas

The Heart Valley is between Spirit River and Grande Prairie up in the Peace River country. It's good land, some of the best farming country in Canada in its own way. But in the stretch where we first looked, and finally settled, the land still open for pre-emption was cut up by big ravines. Maybe sixty acres up on the flat and the rest down in a deep coulee. But more than that it was eighteen miles from town, from the railroad. Hans said, "That's impossible. That's thirty-six miles to town, round trip." By wagon. We didn't dream of owning a truck in them days. "Thirty-six miles of them terrible mud roads, trails. That means almost a whole day trip coming to town." We wanted to find something closer to a town and we heard about land opening up along the Peace River itself.

We started out to hike it. It was over a hundred miles through heavy bush and we never been out in that kind of wilderness before in our lives. I had just a little haversack and Hans had a bag tied up with rope. That and our bedrolls. We went cross-country to the Burnt River and followed it down to the Peace River. That's almost a story in itself. On that trip we got lost and damn near starved to death.

Finally we got to the Peace and got into a fight where we almost killed each other. That was due to the strain we was under. I'd left some ropes behind in the last place we camped. When we got to the Peace we was going to build a raft and float down to Peace River junction. But I got kind of muddled and forgot the ropes so we didn't have anything to tie the logs together with. The Peace is a big river; a good half mile across, maybe more, and a fast moving river. In the end we found an abandoned log house, completely caved in. We pulled some nails out of that cabin. Little two and a half inch nails which we had to straighten out. We tacked our logs together with those nails and drifted down the Peace, trying to steer the raft with some boards we found.

We slowly drifted across. But on the other shore we couldn't get in. There was a current that would keep pushing us out again. Finally we managed to grab hold of the branches of this big tree that had fallen into the river but was still anchored to the bank. We pulled ourselves in on that. There was a house on the top of a bluff not far away. By that time we didn't have anything to eat for three days. We run up to this farmer; neither of us could speak much English. "No eat. No eat. Three days no eat. Hungry, hungry." And he put everything he had on the table and really gave us a feed (laughs). Then we crawled into a straw pile and slept for a day.

Our raft was still tied to the shore with branches. So we got on and drifted down to Peace River town. It took us about two days. During that trip down the Peace we never even seen any land that might be suitable. Because that river has very high banks and any farm land would have been up in the benches, way above us. There was supposed to be land opened up around Bear Lake. But that turned out to be too far out. By that time we were almost ready to give up. So we figured we better file on the first place we looked at in Heart Valley. Peace River town had a land office. Filing a homestead claim was ten dollars then. But by that time we only had ten dollars between the two of us. So we filed on one homestead.

We got back to Wanham, that was the nearest railroad station to our area, and got a job jacking up a grain elevator there. From there we got a job working on the railroad. Like so many immigrants we worked on the railroad, laying track. It was a horrible life. Mosquitoes so thick you could wipe them off in handfuls. Sometimes you couldn't make out the color of the shirt of the guy working in front of you. You'd be just covered with mosquitoes. It was near a place called Woking. There were swamps on both sides of the track. We lived in half a box car with a young couple. Us, that couple and their baby, piles of flour sacks and other supplies in one corner, altogether in half this railway car. Fight off the mosquitoes in the day and have the mice running over you at night. And then try and cook supper and heat water to wash with for four people on this little tin camp stove.

There was about twenty of us repairing track that never had been laid properly. The boss would yell, "Heave ho." Straightening up this old track that was all crooked and tacking it down again. It was one of the toughest jobs I ever done in my life. On account of the mosquitoes and poor living conditions mostly. We worked every day, often twelve hours a day. This whole crew was just come over from Poland and wanted to make as much money as fast as possible so they could get out to farm. We lasted about two months then we was completely wore out.

About the end of August we quit and went down to around Calgary to make some money on the harvest. But the crops were poor and combines were already coming in, so there was very little work around. I managed to get a couple of weeks on a steam threshing gang and that was it. With everything, by the end of September, I had about 150 dollars. That's all the money I had to start homesteading on. There was nothing much else to do so we went back to the Heart Valley.

Peace River Homestead

STARTING OUT

When we got back to Heart Valley my partner filed on his homestead. After that the first thing we did was throw up a shack to get us through the winter. We was very fortunate, because the weather held good and we was able to get up a cabin before it turned cold. Just a very small log hut covered with bark and sod for a roof. That's where me and Hans spent our first homestead year.

After we had the cabin up we started clearing our land—right through the winter. Except for a few periods when it was just too cold. You can frost your lungs doing heavy work outside. We cleared by hand, cutting off the trees first with an axe. The land wasn't heavy bush. It was more like park land with some natural meadows and pastures. We'd chop out the remaining trees on those open spots. Then we made a deal with neighbours who were more established than us. We'd work for them so many days and they'd come with their teams and help us pull out stumps. We didn't have no horses or harness. To start with, we didn't have nothing. A couple of axes, two shovels, a saw; not even a grindstone to sharpen the axe with.

That first winter we damn near lived on rolled oats and corn syrup. We bought five pound pails of Roger's corn syrup and two pound pails of lard. That and the odd moose or deer we got—there was lots of game up there. That's how we survived through the winter. The next family was six miles away. The Michell's, Scotch people, lovely people. The wife would bake bread for us once a week and we would work it off. So once a week we got a big batch of bread from them and the odd pound of butter or cheese or something. We worked that off by helping him clear his place.

Next spring I got a little money from home and I started to homestead in earnest. Up to that time I didn't have animals or anything growing and I didn't feel I'd have my roots down in that land till I had them. I got a pig and one cow and some chickens and I had some money left for seed. I still had to work out about half the time to get things I needed to get started farming.

Pulling out stumps is some job. Of course, nothing like getting these big cedar stumps out down on the coast here (laughs). But it was some terrible hard work even on the land we had in the Peace River. You dig down around the stumps and chop the roots till it's just about loose enough to give. Then you hitch the team up, as high as possible on the stump. They can usually pull it right over and out. But till you get experience it'a very hard on the horses, hard on their shoulders. You snap the ham straps, straps that hold the collar. We had such poor equipment. If you had good equipment and harness and you knew what you're doing it was okay. But what we had was what you call a haywire outfit. It was all put together with little bits of rope and haywire and that sort of thing. We didn't even have a stump puller, we pulled them out directly. Even years later when I was more or less established. Still, that first year I rough cleared about thirty acres, all by hand. That's quite a bit for this type of land.

I worked for neighbours, clearing their land. Then they would come over with their teams and breaking plow and break some my my land. Maybe one day with his team to my two. Money wasn't involved, wasn't available anyway. Every thing was done on a barter arrangement, almost everything. You either worked it out or you found something to trade in exchange.

Breaking land after it was cleared was a very tough job. Somebody came with a team of four, maybe six, horses and what we called a breaking plow. That's a very heavy plow that cuts the sod up and breaks it up some. God, some of that sod was heavy. If the clearing was done poorly, sloppily, there'd be roots and parts of stumps left in. We had to leave some stumps standing because they was too tough to get out at first.

When the breaking plow went into one of these stumps or hit one of the big roots it would get stuck. We had to unhitch the horses, hitch them on the other way and pull the plow out, and then hitch them up in front again. Those poor horses, it was ruthless work. My partner was a farmer in Germany and he'd always taken good care of his horses. We felt terrible about the way we had to drive those horses. But we drove ourselves too, to the point of exhaustion sometimes. Hardly enough to eat that first year. I don't believe in sentimentality about animals, but your animals should be treated with a certain respect and care. We were just too pushed for that.

Many of them horses had big sores on their shoulders from jerking so hard on the harness. We'd wash them out with vinegar. The horses had to be turned out into the bush land. They got very little hay; they were just turned loose to forage. There were natural meadows of pea vine growing there and that stuff makes a wonderful feed. Of course the horses would stray away and you'd often start out in the morning hunting your horses. It might be a couple of hours before you'd find them and bring them back, and then try and get your work in.

We'd built a log barn over on Hans' place. Made of logs with poles on the roof. Some of our neighbours told us, "You put straw on that roof. Like thatch. That's good enough till you get time to fix it up proper." So we hauled five, six loads of straw from a neighbour and put it on the roof. Then they told us, "You have to make a fire yard, because if you don't a prairie fire can come along and burn you out." Right. So we plowed three furrows around the yard and started to back burn the grass to make a firebreak. I thought it was a safe distance away. But that back fire got out of control and burned our barn down, completely. The barn, our straw, the feed oats we'd bought and the harness. But we survived, we kept struggling along (laughs).

How did I learn how to farm? Well, I learned something from my partner. But what he knew from farming in the old country wasn't too much help up in the Peace River. Mostly we learned from what our neighbours were doing, watching what they did and talking to them. Most of them was sort of experimenting too and was only at it a few years more than us. After you picked up some of the basics it was mainly your own experience and practice. Maybe not all the things we done was very wise but over time we changed our methods. We improved and learned what to grow. We raised oats and Garnet, Garnet wheat. That was the only kind that could stand that northern climate. It would stand some frost and not shrivel up. The other varieties they raised further south on the prairie, when they're hit by frost there was nothing left of them. That's the kind of thing you learn right away.

Then too the Peace River country was very generous to us. It was virgin land we was opening up, remember. Never been farmed before. You could make a lot of mistakes and still get by. Get by in the sort of life that we were willing to put up with while we were building up. The winters were rough but never so bad that they discouraged us entirely. Although about March the winter seemed just about endless. But there was enough wood, we could keep warm and comfortable. After the first year we had enough to eat.

Besides, you always thought what that land could do. I mean it was a productive farming area; it wasn't like the dry belt where there's no rain for a while and the land starts drifting and blowing away. You ever see the picture *The Drylanders*? Fabulous film. Well, we never had that.

We always had some crop, even if you couldn't get nothing for it. Even if we froze out or hailed out, there was always something left. It was never as desolate as down in the dry belt prairies around southern Alberta or Saskatchewan. Because even in the worst winter there was always food available for the livestock.

We had these enormous straw stacks. We'd turn the horses loose in the fall and they'd drift around from one straw stack to another and come through the winter fine. The kind of threshing machines we had were very crude and enough grain passed into the straw that the horses and even the cattle wintered well on straight straw. Just some extra oats to keep them around. And cows had to have a barn for the winter.

We grew very little hay at that time. What with those straw stacks and pawing down through the snow to get forage the horses did fine. We had a wonderful growth up there. Pea vine; it belongs to the Vetch family. I never seen it any other place. It grows wild there in the natural meadows. It grew higher than a cow, the cattle would disappear in it. Endless meadows of this pea vine. We used to cut it for hay. It beats alfalfa by a long shot, very high in protein and it dries really beautifully.

There were other things we had in plenty. We always had moose meat. I didn't go hunting myself but there was always somebody who'd give you a hind quarter or a half a moose. We ate so much moose meat we got sick of it. If you eat too much of it it gives you diarrhea. Later on I raised some pigs and started making my own ham and bacon.

Gradually you get some money here and there. But whatever money you get you put into equipment and horses. Whatever you can grow or make yourself you make. And it's amazing what you can make for yourself, and repair, if you're determined. Nothing got thrown out, you always find some use for it sooner or later. You start raising your own horses and other animals and then you're on your way. Slowly you build up your whole farm. And that's what happened in the whole area.

But like I said, we was fortunate. That was good land we were farming. We struck that land mainly by luck. There was some areas badly burnt over, where the top soil was all gone. Some areas the soil was no good to start with. People settled in them places not having sufficient experience or not having any choice. Most of these people who got in those areas had to pull out after struggling for four, five years. Time and time again nothing would grow. The C.P.R. brought in people to settle enormous blocks of land that was completely unsuitable for farming. Sold it to these settlers. And they had to leave it after building homes and struggling for years until the realization came to them, "This land is completely hopeless to make a living from."

I was spared all that because where we settled the soil was wonderful; absolutely incredible. Productive? Some raised up to 105 bushels of oats, which was close to the record. Yes, right, 105 bushels of oats per acre. I myself once got 98 bushel oats. On new land I raised up to sixty bushels of wheat, which was completely fantastic. Forty bushels Garnet wheat per acre was quite common. And that's a darn good crop. On the prairies if they got twenty bushels per acre they're talking about a bumper crop. We more than doubled that in our part of the Peace River. When you get crops like that it makes an awful lot of difference, it makes your struggle meaningful and bearable because you can see the results.

BUILDING UP

I wanted a mixed farm. I was committed to that from the very beginning. Animals were a part of farm life for me. Not everybody felt that way, especially the farmers that come up from the prairies. Many of them was strictly grain farmers. They didn't want an animal around, they wanted a tractor. Throw in a crop and take it off and that's it. But I built up a mixed farm, what you could call a family farm. The Peace River and those times were more suitable to mixed farming than straight one-crop farming.

I made up my mind I didn't want any scrub. I wanted good foundation stock and went out and looked for that. One neighbour had a good herd and I picked out an animal that I thought was top breeding stock. I said, "I'd like to buy that cow." He says, "No, I'm keeping her." So I offered him a price that was far above market value. He told me later that he thought I was a complete greenhorn to offer that price and he didn't want to take it at first. But then he just couldn't resist, especially when I offered cash. I got an outstanding animal. I bought more cows later but she was the best one I ever had. She built the foundation of my herd.

One of the most wonderful things about that life up there was the neighbours we had. Always helpful and not closing anybody out. For instance, nobody had fire insurance. There was no such thing and nobody could afford it anyway. The only security that you had was living with your neighbours. And they would look after you in an emergency. Of course everybody pulled their weight too.

I recall, one New Year's night, we went to a dance the other side of the creek. The whole district was there. About midnight a fire broke out in a farm about two, three miles down the road. The family was at the community hall dancing when somebody comes running into the hall yelling, ''Fire, fire.'' Everybody rushed down but by the time we got there there was nothing left but ashes. That was on the first of January, in the Peace River, where it's down to thirty to forty below. By four o'clock that morning the hall was packed with everything anybody could spare—blankets, pots and pans, food, furniture. Everything to set this family up again. And a couple of days later the men got together and started cutting logs to build them a new home. By the middle of March that house was finished and they moved back in. Maybe you don't know what that means, building in the dead of winter. But that's something. And the most magnificent thing about it was that everybody went over and pitched in and done what he could do. Everybody just helped as they could, with no big organization or committees.

In the same manner we built a community hall, and held dances and concerts. I even wrote a play and acted in it, yes sir (laughs). Basically, it was a good life. Because people learned to cooperate. They were maybe not all the best of friends, like in any other place, but they knew they depended on each other and they helped each other out when it was needed. And that's good. That forces you to appreciate, or at least to understand, the other people around you. Even if you have some friction sometimes and feel like saying, ''To hell with him.''

That necessity to cooperate starts to disappear, I think, when people get money and when they have machinery to get by more or less on their own. It's most lamentable, in my estimation.

What can be a danger in these homestead areas, what can be destructive in a way, is the obsession to build up the farm.

There's always some work that should be done. You never are completely caught up. If you let it, that constant work becomes your whole life. I seen that happen often enough. In our district we were fortunate. For a pioneering community, we led a comparatively active social life. At least in the winter. We made our own music. There was always some reading material available. But not all districts were that lucky. In some settlements the only entertainment they had was the church.

In some of those communities the church played a very powerful role. Maybe even a beneficial role, sometimes. Because it brought people together. But to my way of thinking it was a very poor way to do it. There were communities where almost everybody was Ukrainian or Mennonite or from one church or another. If you weren't part of that group you had a pretty tough time. Our district was pretty mixed right from the beginning. There were some English families and Scotch. There were a bunch of Germans and some Norwegians and Swedes. All sorts of different people came along later. That made it possible for all of us to feel like we were part of a new, a wider group. One minister from the prairies tried to set up a German community of his own church there, but thank God it broke up. The church was never very successful in our area.

We were already feeling very strongly Canadian after a couple of years. It never occurred to me for a minute that I would want to go back to Germany after I started homesteading. That was it. I wanted to build a home here and live here and farm here. I never questioned, I don't think I ever questioned that decision. Most of us, five years after we had landed, we had taken out our citizenship papers. We felt, due to this pioneering, we felt very much Canadian. We felt we were part of building up Canada. In other parts of the country it might not have been so easy to feel that.

Although I bached for four years I was completely committed to the idea that I would eventually marry and have a family up in the Peace River. That was true of almost all of us. We were all bachelors up there, except for a few of the English homesteaders who had come out with their families.

Us bachelors were all desperate—you can use the word "desperate" quite properly here—we were desparate to get a wife one way or the other (laughs).

Everybody tried in his own way to find a wife and to get a family started. Each guy wrote to his girlfriend, if he had one, or to a whole list of girlfriends, seeing if one would come up and marry him. Then he wrote to his relatives to see if they knew of anybody. Some guys would write to every girl they'd ever known in the old country to see if one would be willing to come over and marry them. There was darn few marriageable girls to be picked up in those new homestead areas. As soon as they were sixteen or seventeen they already had a whole string of young bachelors calling on them. They got proposals like hot cakes.

Eventually, by hook and crook, the boys all managed to get wives to come up there. That was done almost all by mail. Very few of them went out of the area to do their courting. During those years everything was done without any of us leaving the area. We just didn't have the money or time. People came in from outside, but hardly any of us went out, even for short trips.

In my own case, I first asked a girlfriend I had had in Germany to come over and marry me. But she wouldn't even consider living on a farm. So I brooded for about a year or so. It struck me that it was stupid to ask somebody that I knew from a completely different life. So I started to write to Hilde, the girl I valued most and who I thought would suit this type of life best. For a long time I couldn't get up the nerve to ask her. Finally I wrote to Hilde and she agreed to come over. Thank goodness I married her.

At that time you had to deposit two hundred and fifty dollars with the government to bring a prospective bride over; for return fare in case you didn't get married. That would be 1932, in July. I had to borrow money for the fare and that deposit. When your bride got to Grande Prairie you damn nearly took her off the train and straight to the minister and got married on the spot so you could get your two hundred and fifty dollars back. Which you desperately needed to pay back your debts or buy some equipment or something.

Those marriages worked out very well in most cases. In most cases they worked out at least as well as these romantic affairs, which burn out after a year or so anyway. Maybe I have some peculiar ideas about marriage. I lean much more to the idea of marriages where people decide they are going to learn to live together and develop an affection for each other. They are a much more sensible base than these over-exaggerated romantic theatricals played up by Hollywood.

By the time Hilde came over I had built a very nice little log house. I bought some lumber for the floor and the logs are what you called hewed. You flatten the side of the logs with a broadaxe. Kind of rough, because good broadaxe work takes years of practice. But it looked pretty nice any way and was a very solid house. I'd even bought a new stove and made some pieces of furniture, like a big bed (chuckles). I attempted to modernize the place so that some of the drudgery of homestead life would be eliminated for Hilde. We never got electricity but I made wash tubs and a sink. Yes sir, we even had a bath tub. None of those other homesteads had that—very up to date (laughs).

The trouble always was that there just was no cash to buy things we couldn't produce. We always had lots of food—meat, milk, and butter. I would take some of our wheat to the mill and have it ground to make our own flour. We used wheat for our breakfast food. Used to put it in stone crocks and let it swell overnight and then cook it for breakfast. Makes an excellent breakfast food in my opinion.

Our grocery bill was very slim. But you have to have sugar and syrup, salt, spices. We also had to have coffee, which I guess isn't essential. There are some things that aren't absolutely essential but necessary. Because if you want them and can't have them you feel like you must be doing very poorly. We planted sugar beets and tried to make our own sugar and syrup. But that was just too much trouble. There are little things that you need in groceries even if you produce all your own food. As I recall, we could get by with a twenty-five dollar grocery bill from fall till springtime. In the spring, the store would extend us credit till next harvest. That used to be another twenty dollars, spring till fall. Besides that there was coal oil and nails and clothes or a replacement for some tool that you absolutely could not repair anymore. Altogether I don't think we laid out more than a hundred dollars cash on goods most of those years we lived there.

We had one really bad year. The year after Hilde and I got married. The grain was just headed out when, overnight, the weather dropped to below freezing. Next morning my whole field was snow white, absolutely frozen. No crop of any kind left. So I had to go out to work. I rode away and left Hilde at home to take care of the animals we had. I had to make enough cash to get us through the winter. Once winter set in in that area there'd be no wage work of any kind.

Frost just hits certain strips, it depends upon the moisture content of the air. It moves in a belt maybe a few miles wide and up to a hundred miles long. I went over to another district about thirty miles away and made a little money cutting hay and worked for a farmer threshing. My wages came to forty dollars, which would have carried us through the winter. But he wouldn't, or couldn't pay up. I had to ride over there three times in the middle of winter till I got most of my wages. Somehow Hilde and me got through that winter, which was the worst year we had in the Peace River.

Whatever you could possibly spare you traded off for something you really needed. Those were getting to be really tight times then, in the early thirties. I once traded off a whole litter of pigs, close to nine hundred pounds, for an old hay rake. And I thought that was a pretty good trade too. We done a great deal on a neighbourly basis. We even worked off our taxes building roads in that area. There wouldn't of been no money to pay taxes anyway. You'd spend a month working on the roads.

Whatever money we did get for our crops went to build up the farm. Everything was sacrificed to get machinery (horse drawn machinery) and horses and harness. To get log chains and some tools and other necessary equipment. Always something more or some replacement was needed, and that came before needs of a more personal nature. This went on year after year. Of course it was not so grim as it might sound because it was very rewarding to us to see the farm building up. But in all the years we were in the Peace River we never had a radio. That really is terrible now that I think of it.

But there was a big difference between all of us and those young people going out from the cities today looking to live on the land. We never had any intention or desire to do without material things. We were always hoping and dreaming to have things. We wanted a nice home and all that goes with it. Later on we wanted a car. We worked for those things and slaved for them and sacrificed to build up. And we were certain we'd have them in the end.

I think what was involved for me was that I wanted to get those things on my own. I don't know if it comes through very clearly in what I been saying, but I wanted to prove myself. This is very important. I wanted to satisfy myself that I could provide for myself and my own family, building right from scratch.

WHY WE LEFT

When the depression set in the prices dropped down something fierce. Wheat dropped to twenty cents at the elevator—around 1933 or so. Yes, that's right—a bushel of wheat for twenty cents. Raised, harvested, threshed, and delivered to the elevator over eighteen miles of mud road. When I bought oats for seed in 1928 they was running close to sixty cents a bushel. Even that was a low price. But in 1934, oats was bringing as low as six cents a bushel, delivered. If you could get somebody to buy them

The pressures of the market, even up there, pushed you from pillar to post, from one crop to another. At first it was wheat, wheat was what was wanted. Then with the depression and the flooded market wheat became almost valueless. The time came when they burned wheat acreages down in the States and shovelled wheat into fire boxes in steam engines because it was cheaper than any other fuel. So you try barley, or flax and feed grains or something. We always managed to sell a little, get some cash. But if we hadn't been so self-sufficient up there most of us wouldn't have survived.

I don't think anybody today can realize how isolated we was up there then. Now you can get on a train here in Vancouver and you're up there in eighteen, twenty hours. Or you just drive up or fly up, and never think anything of it. They get the same news and the same advertising over television in every farm house that we get here, at the same time. But in those days we were very much cut off from the world. I never felt isolated up there, but we were. News from the outside sort of drifted in. None of our neighbours had a radio. There was no telephone. We got mail once a week. I subscribed to a weekly newspaper and that was our main link to the outside world. I got the *Free Press Prairie Farmer* and along with that you got *The Family Herald*, coming out of Winnipeg.

I done a lot of reading. But not much about current events. I was very naive about politics at that time. In some ways maybe I still am. I read about Hitler coming to power in Germany. We got some reports, letters from our friends and relatives still over there. There was little about all that in the Canadian newspapers. But it wasn't until we came down to Vancouver that I really begun to understand what was going on.

The only thing I was active in politically was the United Farmers of Alberta. But even then we was all very—'naive' is the only word I can think of. This Aberhardt, the preacher, came along in the middle of the depression and promised that if Social Credit won the election (in Alberta) they'd distribute a bonus of twenty-five dollars a month to every family. To stimulate the economy, to get things rolling. That was *the* social credit. Whatever we thought of Aberhardt or Social Credit everybody thought that was just dandy. Our area voted for Social Credit over eighty percent. I did too (laughs). Of course there never was any sign of that money.

While I was generally happy with homesteading life I came to realize that it was a terrible life for Hilde. She liked lots of company and it was a joyless life for her. A rather lonely life.

All building up the farm and very little real joy from day to day. Very little to stimulate her, no music or anything. You'd come home often exhaused. The seasons were very short. You worked tremendously long hours once seeding started, as long as you and the horses stood up. That went on most of the summer and even more so during threshing time, because every day counted. In the winter there was more time, but there was still the daily grind of doing chores; melting water, hauling grain, feeding stock, in that twenty below weather. Always something to be done. For a fact, I'd say I seen only one woman who seemed perfectly content with that life. All the rest felt the lack of one thing or another in time and wanted to get out.

The men were working to build up the farm and they were creating something they could see. But the women missed out on that and also didn't have any of the niceties of life; they had nothing. The men were involved in building up while the women only participated in the background of running the farm.

Don't get me wrong, women worked hard on the farm too. Cooking, taking care of the house, helping with the garden and doing chores. And some pretty tough things, too. Hilde many times rode over and brought back the breeding bull, that colossally big bull weighing close to a ton. He had a ring in his nose and Hilde brought him behind her saddle horse, through the ravines, over to the cows. That takes some guts I'll tell you. I was too busy with other things and it had to be done, so Hilde would go and get the bull. That was all there was to it. Women had that stamina. Naturally not all women would do that or could do that, but she did.

But there was so many of the niceties lacking. Hilde always loved music. But I traded off her guitar for something or other that I needed desperately. I was going to get her a second hand piano as soon as I got ahead of the game a bit. But I never did; I couldn't, for twenty years.

That reminds me of a remarkable book I read recently. The name escapes me now; a typical pioneering story. How this man never had time for his family. How he's always going to go on a picnic with them or take them on a holiday but always some problem comes up and he can't because there's work that has to be done. Never enough money for any luxuries or little additional things. Finally, after many years of struggle he manages to build a new house and puts a piano in it. His wife goes in and sits down at the piano and says, "Now it's too late, I'm burned out."

Over time I come to the realization that this wasn't the life for Hilde. If we would have had children it might have been different. We would have been tied down anyway and maybe life would have been more complete. If you had children you could eventually pass what you'd built up on to them. Of course it's not like that today either. Most farm kids can't hardly wait to get off the farm. But in them days the farm was always intended as a family affair. But we just didn't have any children. Not because we didn't try often enough, it just never seemed to take (laughs).

Sickness was an awful thing if it should strike you, or a serious accident. That's what everybody was always afraid of. Because there was no medical insurance, no bank account, and no security behind you. You lived in fear that an accident would happen to you or your wife would fall sick. That's what happened to us. In the winter of 1935 I think. I got so crippled up with sciatica that for weeks all I could do was sit in a chair. I couldn't even sleep. All the work was thrown on Hilde.

The neighbours were wonderful. You would hardly believe how they jumped in and done everything for us. They came over every day and did the heavy chores. Finally they brought out the public health nurse. She was a lady doctor actually, working as a nurse then. A marvellous person. She said, "Face it. You can't go on like that. You've got to go to the hospital and have an operation." I told her I didn't have any money. "Don't worry about money. We'll fix you up. We'll get you into the hospital somehow. You've got to have that operation." She even sent out her own gramaphone and records for me to pass the time.

About a week later the neighbours loaded me into a covered sleigh and took me the sixty miles to Grande Prairie, to the hospital. I had the operation and when I was well

72

enough to travel some other neighbours made that long trip down to bring me back. In the meantime everything was in good hands. They done all the chores and looked after my cattle. No money changed hands. That cooperation and neighbourliness was all you had to rely on. I don't know if most people can even understand what this means today.

But all these things, the sciatica, not being able to sell what we produced, and most of all the realization that this isolation was no good for Hilde, made me decide to pick up and make a new start in B.C. Over time, most of the people in that district left their farms too. That happened a bit later and was partly due to the economics of modernization and expansion. But families left, one by one. The kids had to go to school in one of the towns if they wanted to go past grade five. Having kids living in town created a stress on the budget. Sooner or later the wives mostly wanted to live in town.

Today it's completely different up there. Almost nobody lives in that area. They mainly live in Grande Prairie and drive out to farm in the springtime and for the harvest. Most of them farms where our neighbours lived, there's nothing—no animals, no people. In that area where we lived, where there were over thirty families, there's maybe five or six families living now. All the rest are gone.

Work and Wages

A SORT OF TREK

We had a fairly good crop in 1936 but the price was so low that all the wheat and cattle we sold still gave us nothing. That fall we finally decided to leave and try our luck down on the coast. During that winter and spring I made what arrangements I could and got together whatever money I could. I didn't sell the farm, you couldn't sell it. I rented out the land on a share basis to one of my neighbours. I sold all the livestock and cattle, the horses, the machinery, most of everything in our house. It's impossible to describe how I felt. We just took a few suitcases and some boxes of clothes and kitchen utensils. Ten years of work building up that homestead into a farm, and a relatively successful one, too, and we got almost nothing. Cattle was next to worthless, two cents a pound on the hoof. We got less than three hundred dollars for everything and I think that included my last grain check too.

I bought a second hand car up there, which was an enormous mistake. Because driving it out from the Peace River used up most of our money. It's a long story and I don't know if I should go into it. Well, okay.

The beginning of April, 1937. We tried to get out on the frost, while the frost was still in the ground. During break-up you just could not get through those roads in a car. But we waited just a little too long. The frost was out of the ground and there were frost holes eight, ten inches deep and mud up to the axles in many places. I don't know how many times we had to get some guy with a team of horses to pull us out of a mud hole. We got as far as Grande Prairie but we couldn't get across the Smoky River. The melt water was on the ice two feet deep. The ice was still underneath it but I didn't have the guts to try driving across it. No bridge of course. So we had to stay in a motel for more than a week, till the ferry was running, and that cost a mighty penny.

We still had to drive that hundred and fifty miles to Edmonton over a road that was just one long pot hole. Hardly ever got out of first gear. That burnt the motor right out of the car and we hardly got to Edmonton. It cost me ninety dollars to have that engine overhauled and rebuilt, which was an enormous amount of money to us at that time. We had only sixty, seventy dollars left to get to the coast. It was like a nightmare, where you run and run but barely move, while something is coming up behind you.

I managed to get a job on a big farm near Edmonton. I drove a big rig called a tiller combine and did fallowing during the summer. Hilde and me lived there and saved every cent of my pay, which was very little. After the harvest we set off for B.C. again. Drove down to Calgary and made it into B.C. on the old road through the pass. Mile after mile of washboard. The old car shook and shook and shook itself to pieces. It shook the shims out of the spokes, wooden spokes, and we had to get a new set of wheels.

You had to dip down through the States, because that road didn't go through all the way to the coast. We come to Spokane, Washington, and there I see asphalt road for the first time in the trip. So I opened the car wide up and we're travelling along at thirty miles an hour (laughs). It almost seemed we was flying. The next thing I know all my tires are worn out because the steering and suspension was completely shot. I had to buy a new set of tires, which was another big shock.

That same night we parked in a peach orchard just outside Wenatchee. It must have been the beginning of October and most of that fruit was never picked. We slept in the car and all night long peaches dropped around us and right on top of the car. It was a terrific experience and I almost thought we'd come to the land of milk and honey.

We came down to the coast with the idea of farming. I was hoping I would find a small piece of farm land here and put a down payment on it with the money I'd get selling the place up in the Peace River. I didn't realize the conditions were completely different on the coast. Land prices were ten, twenty times higher than in the Peace River. I never even got to seriously look at a farm, let alone buy one. For the next few years we were completely broke. We were completely stranded.

When we hit Vancouver I discovered that the block in the car was split. I didn't have the money to have it repaired so I sold the car for about twenty-five dollars. Besides that we had another twenty dollars left over. That's all we brought out of the Peace River, for ten years of work.

NO RELIEF

The second day we're in Vancouver we went over to see Otto. He was a good friend of Hilde's brother over in the old country. Otto and Grete were living in a big basement apartment in one of the rooming houses that used to be where the B.C. Hydro building is now. They were paying, I think, nine dollars a month for rent for that place. Otto was unemployed so we decided it would make sense if we pooled what we had. We chipped in on the rent and moved in with them.

Vancouver is where I really got to know what the depression meant. Up in the Peace River, well it was much like any homestead area at any time. There was no work whatever in Vancouver. I looked and looked. Walked to every factory, every hiring agency I could find. Went day after day. There were big signs on all these places—"No Men Wanted." God, some of those guys working in the front office were arrogant. After a while, after going around every day, you got to feel, "What's the use?" Because you saw so many other guys doing the same thing and never getting anywhere.

About that time there was an (B.C. provincial) election and these great big signs come up, right on Granville Street—"Work and Wages." There'll be work for everyone. All that B.S. endlessly repeated. It was this Patullo. They was going to build highways and things, a highway to the Peace River. I thought of that many times, years later. Many times when I crossed the Patullo bridge. I remembered clearly how I went home to Hilde and said, "Now there'll be work. They promised us." I was still that innocent (laughs). Well, maybe not so innocent as desparate to believe it. Of course, nothing happened. It was just election time.

Grete would get the occasional job as house helper. She'd get maybe twenty cents an hour, two, three hours work a day. Otto was conducting the Swedish male choir. He was a professional musician and sometimes he got the occasional engagement where he played with a dance band. Things was very, very tight. But that place where they lived was always full of people. We had lots of leisure and more company and talk than I ever had before or since. A lot of it was just pipe dreaming though; talk in place of not being able to do something.

We'd chip in and get a one pound tin of tobacco. Otto had this little machine that rolled cigarettes. He would be sitting there rolling cigarettes and we'd all be sitting around drinking coffee and smoking and planning how to get some money, talking all night. We sat around every night thinking up new schemes—we were going to bake stuff and sell it house to house (laughs). The most crazy schemes. We even thought about robbing banks. But we never done anything, nothing ever materialized. And eventually I wound up in the relief camps.

What happened to me personally was that I always felt I had to work. Even if we'd been able to get relief, which we couldn't, I couldn't just sit around. After you've worked all those years it's just like hell to sit around and do nothing. I figured any work would be better than that. God those times were terrible.

We was completely out of money and I didn't want to live off Otto and Grete. They didn't have it anyway. So we moved out. Hilde got a job as a live-in maid. Room and board and not much more. She couldn't even tell her employer that she was married; otherwise they wouldn't hire her. If we wanted to lay together like a man and wife we had to go to Stanley

77

Park and crawl into the bushes on her day off. Because we didn't have the price of a hotel room where we could spend the night together.

The whole time I was in Vancouver I got one day's work, wheeling concrete. I got a few days work out in the Fraser Valley with one farmer.

Finally, I got on at the relief project camp at Green Timbers. That was still out in the countryside then. It was a forestry project. The only way I could get into that camp was on a fictitious name. The name I used was Wilmer, Abe Wilmer. To get into one of those camps you had to be in B.C. for at least a year. But I'd only been here four months or so.

There was a Provincial policeman that checked you out before they let you in the camp. "Where you been living," he says. "I been homesteading up in Rolla." That's in B.C., just across the line from where I lived. Maybe thirty, forty miles away. "Who's the storekeeper up in Rolla?" he asks me. "Oh," I say,"that's Henry." I never been in Rolla (laughs). "Henry what?" "I don't know his other name. I don't know the second name of a lot of people," I says. That was true, because you could know people for a long time and never know their second name. "Well, where'd you live?" he says. "Oh, I lived in the bush, eight miles down the road." By that time he knew what it was about, that I was from across the border in Alberta. But I got in.

There were about a hundred and twenty men living in tents there. We slashed a road through the brush and planted trees and made fireguards and dug ditches. We made about twenty-six cents a day. Not an hour, but twenty-six cents per day. Magnificent, eh? We didn't work very hard and we didn't really accomplish anything.

That was one of the terribly demoralizing things about those projects. They were just pointless make-work schemes. Like when we were making a road. The boys knew damn well that with a truck and a tractor, a dozen men could have done what maybe a hundred men with wheelbarrows and pick and shovel did. Besides, you were cut off from the outside world. That was especially tough for those that had a wife. They gave you room and board and light work and for that you accepted living in a sort of jail. Your life was just wasted. That was it. We sat in camp desperately hoping to hear of some real job or come up with some solution. But you were stuck there.

I stayed at Green Timbers for three months, till April (1938). I got to be the local secretary of the Relief Project Workers Association there. That wasn't very well supported by the men either, regretably. Even though they were all down and out. Still very individualistic after all that. "Next spring I'm going to get out of here and get a job somewhere. It's going to pick up then. I don't need this sort of association to back me up." All sorts of baloney like that.

Partly, that's what them camps did. As long as some guys had a warm bed and meals and a little money for tobacco they were completely apathetic. We'd call a meeting and maybe eight or ten guys would turn up. We'd go around from one tent to another. "Come on boys, you been bitching about the conditions here. Well, come on to the meeting and we'll decide what to do." Then maybe twenty or twenty-five would turn up out of that whole camp.

In April we decided we was all going to pull out of that camp. For what specific reason I don't remember now. I think most of the boys from other camps (they were scattered all over the Valley and even in the interior), most of them pulled out and came into Vancouver. That was the time you could stand down at the docks and see the freight trains come in, every train loaded with men riding on top.

But those conditions pressed you to start thinking politically. It makes people ready to join parties. Lots of people I knew in Vancouver were supporters of the Communist Party. A lot of the Swedes I knew were pretty left. A lot of people from different backgrounds in fact. Some joined the Party. Although it wasn't all that strong even then. Never been strong in Canada in fact. But at least it was active trying to do something instead of dishing out more baloney. So for a while I joined the Party too. I don't even remember how that come about, it was so long ago. I wanted to join. I don't think I was recruited in any way. By that time I was good and ready for it. I wanted to be part of something that was doing something. I certainly thought that that was the right thing to do at the time.

All that I can remember is that the people in my group, ten or twelve of us, were some of the most devoted people I ever met. They were deeply concerned to improve things. And they were also disciplined people. They weren't just the sort of parlour discussion group that I seen so often. I respected them very much.

That's the time I went out collecting for one thing or another; for the Relief Project Workers, and the volunteers in Spain. I remember going up and down the streets with a jam tin. Going down Powell and Cordova and all through that area, from store to store. All those little stores used to give something. Ten cents or so; a quarter was a big contribution. Actually they were more generous than anywhere else.

The Relief Project Workers asked the City Council for permission to have a tag day. So we could collect money openly on the street without being arrested. Just one day. We were trying to get the government to turn the camps into public works projects and pay minimum wages. But the (Vancouver) City Council turned us down flat. "No tag day. Them men have got to leave town," they said. The police were supposed to put all the relief camp workers on the freights and get them out of town. Get them going anywhere. So long as they left town. That's when that sit-down strike in the Post Office was organized, that's what brought it on. Personally I think they were 100 per cent right.

UNDERGROUND

I wasn't in that occupation myself because just before it began I managed to get a job. Ali knew somebody who was hiring for a new mine opening up near Nicola Lake. I desperately wanted a job. That's how I slowly lost contact with what was going on in Vancouver. That, I think, was the way it was with the majority of people who drifted away from Party activity. It wasn't that you had some fight with them. It was just that some personal change in your life took place that made it hard to stay involved with what you were doing before.

I never been in a mine in my life before that. But I said I worked in them before, in the old country. "Oh sure, I'm experienced." That was the typical thing to do. Not all these papers and diplomas you have today. If you could bluff your way through the first few days you could usually get the hang of most jobs.

So I got this job up at Stump Lake Mine in the Nicola Valley. It must have been the summer of 1938. For the first four months I was working above ground, pick and shovel work building the crusher and sheds. I wasn't any more an active member of the Party but I still kept in contact and they sent me the *Miners Union* newspaper. That mine didn't have no union. For a fact, there was very few organized unions outside the cities then. They tried in a few camps and mines but always got busted. As far as I remember unions really only took hold later; during the war and even later.

I had this *Miners Union* paper arrive for me in the mail. It was all wrapped up so nobody could see what it was. The superintendent there was just a promoter who didn't know nothing about mining himself. Somehow this Colonel Fell found out I was doing a little agitating among these miners. He says, "I want that man fired. He's an agitator." But what happened was one of the most astonishing and gratifying things I ever seen. We had this foreman who really run the show from a mining standpoint. He was not politically minded at all, in fact I think he was pretty conservative if anything. He says to Fell, "This man is doing his job as well as any man I ever had and he is not going to be fired. I don't believe in that. His ideas are his own business. If he goes, I go." And Fell backed down.

Actually, they didn't have anything to worry about from me because hardly any of those miners could understand me or read the paper. Most were Yugoslavs and hardly spoke any English. They picked up a bit of English after a while. Later on, when the camp got bigger there were about thirty men there. Up to fifty sometimes. Yugoslavs, Austrian guys, a few others from the old country and about ten guys born here in Canada. Most of them all had experience in mines somewhere before.

After a few months I got a job underground. That paid a little more than straight labourer. God that was a haywire little mine. I was underground about six, seven months. First I was tramming, hand tramming. You've seen pictures of them little ore cars coming out of the mine shaft pulled by an electric locomotive? Well I did that, but by hand. Like they did a hundred years ago. Not even horses. I'd push that bloody tram, one ton ore and that steel cart, up to the spill. You get on the slightest grade and you have to push your guts out to make the tram move. Boy, what I suffered with that job.

The worst was loading them cars from the chutes. Inside the mine are these chutes. They run down from another level and are filled with ore. You position your car exactly under the chute. These chutes were pretty poorly built, too. You'd pry it open—no gate or anything, just a big plank wedged in. Then the ore would rush down into your car. Sometimes a big rock gets stuck and you can't get the plank back in. The ore runs over the car, over the track, and you've got to clean that out before you can do anything else.

Then when you finally get to the surface and push that car over to the dump you've got to be careful that she doesn't jump the track. The rails on the dump are just loosely tacked down and jump around. You've got to tie the car down with a logging chain before you dump it so that it doesn't go down the hill; ore, car and all. Once in a while that would happen and then there'd be hell to pay. And all this was done under pressure. You couldn't take your time. I always been very clumsy when I'm under that kind of pressure. Those trams would lock on me and wouldn't do what they were supposed to.

After that I worked with a gang, mucking. Not like they do now, with a machine, but all by hand. You work there, hours at a time, just shovelling the ore away from the face—where they earlier blasted. As soon as you finished loading one car they pull up another one. The only light you see is from those little lamps we wore on our helmets. Backbreaking work. And I been used to hard work by that time. The only good thing about that mine was that she was a dry mine. We never

82

had to worry about water and seepage.

I never did get to like that mining. But after I was underground a while it didn't bother me too much. Of course you always worry a bit, from a timber slipping or a rock fall or somebody getting careless. I think what I was worried about most was getting my foot caught and having one of those cars go over it.

Oh God you sweated there. After work you went right from the shaft to the wash room and had a hot shower. At least they had that. It was like coming out of a long steam bath. You pulled your ordinary clothes down from the ceiling, changed, and went home. After the shower you'd feel tired but kind of good. Sort of light headed.

After about four months I brought Hilde up from Vancouver. There was a sort of shanty town not too far away. Mainly abandoned houses where some Chinese crew had lived a long time ago. They were in a terrible shape. Structurally still okay, but broken down and full of mess where men had camped. Me and Hilde moved into one of them shacks, cleaned it up and fixed it up a bit and lived there for about nine months. It was quite homey.

We never got ahead of the game though because every little while they'd close the mine down for a spell. That would set us back. This promoter, Colonel Fell, would come up from Vancouver and bring a car load of fish (prospective suckers) with him. He'd invite anybody from the area that seemed like they had a little money to invest. Fell would lay out a big spread for them and then go into his spiel. It was like a fairy tale. How this was going to be another Bridge River, they were going to build a big mill, the nearby towns would be booming.

SUMMER, 1939

In the thirteen months I worked there we was able to save about a hundred dollars, and we lived very sparingly too. Finally we went back down to the Fraser Valley. It was strawberry time, May or June (1939). Times were still really tough. Did you ever hear those stories about how the depression was really over in '37 or '38? Well it wasn't. It went right on until the war started.

We picked strawberries all over the Fraser Valley and made about a dollar a day. Hilde and me bought a couple of old bicycles and travelled all over the Valley with our bedrolls and packs strapped on the back. Then we picked raspberries. I remember one place we picked; there were about twenty school girls working there. We took it more as a holiday because you sure couldn't make anything at it. We only worked until about four o'clock in the afternoon and then we went swimming in a little river nearby. All day long while we were picking we'd be singing away. Old favorites like *Juanita* and what not. It was very nice. The demoralizing thing about it was that there was never any hope in sight that you could build your future up again. Gradually you got so that you lived from day to day.

We had our sleeping bags along and air mattrresses. We slept anywhere we happened to be at night. We took the money we earned berry picking, twenty or thirty dollars, and we went to Harrison Lake. Spent a whole week living in a cabin, which cost us eight dollars a week and what we thought was enormously expensive. We boarded ourselves, went swimming every day and had a glorious time. When our money was used up we took our bicycles and went out looking for work and wound up in the hop yards around Sardis. Hop picking started in August.

Each family got a little windowless cabin and straw bedding. Those cabins are still there today, although I don't know if they still use them. Many of the people picking there got diarrhea really bad, from who knows what. The water I suppose. Hilde and I averaged about a dollar a day picking. I got hop poisoning in my hands and they swelled up to almost twice their normal size. I still got the knobs on my hands today from that. But I kept on picking.

By that time we was just living from day to day. God, but it's strange. I can see very clearly what we did but I can't remember at all what we felt or thought. I think now that we must have given up thinking about a lot of things that wasn't immediately in front of us. We must have known what was going on in Europe. But I don't remember there being very much talk about it. No, that couldn't be, could it? I know a few years later on I read a great deal about what was going on and I was terribly shocked and depressed. But I have a feeling that that was later, not at the time it was happening. But near the end of the depression I was completely played out, almost in a state of shock.

I remember the day the war broke out. I remember the boss of that hop yard came running down through the yard where we was picking and yelling, "There's going to be a war. There's going to be a war. I got to go buy sugar." And he went to Chilliwack and bought hundred pound bags of sugar. That's what the war meant to him.

Stump Ranching and Camp Work

FORTY STUMPS PER ACRE

I made up my mind that we would go and look for homestead land in southern B.C. somewhere. We was always on the look out for a homestead somewhere but they were hard to find in B.C. by that time. You would have to go way out, often into areas worse than the Peace River. Anyway, I went to the government land office in Abbotsford and got some land maps of the areas around the edge of the Fraser Valley. I discovered that there was a block of land open on a pre-emption back of Cultus Lake, in the Columbia Valley. I went up there and found one pretty good piece of a hundred acres. Somebody had filed on it before as a homestead but then let it go. There was a government claim of $450 against it for improvements, which was totally beyond my means.

I was talking to this one farmer there, saying how I'd like to file on that section but didn't have the money. He says, "I think that you can get them to drop that claim because that improvement was done years ago and it's all grown back into bush now. Why don't you write and tell them that it's depreciated and of no value anymore?" So that's what I done. I filed on the land, just ten dollars, and sent them a letter saying why I thought the assessment was of no value. They knocked that price off and I got the land as a homestead. Of course, I had to prove up on it again. But that was fine. And that's how I got started again in B.C.

I didn't know exactly how we was going to get started. We were flat broke and we didn't have the most simple tools to start homesteading. Just then, just at the right time, a grain check for a hundred dollars comes down from the Peace

River. That was the first money I'd seen out of that place since we left. We had a little tent and our bedding and some clothes. I bought an axe and a crosscut saw, hammers, a shovel, wedges, and some grub and we set out for our new place.

I found a great big cedar log laying off the ground near where we was planning to build a shack. I didn't think nothing about it because I was from the prairies. But one neighbour comes over and says, "Man, are you lucky. You got enough cedar in there to build your whole house." I said, "You got to be kidding. There's already little trees growing out of the top." "No sir," he says. "That's good cedar, top old growth cedar." And so it was. We cut long bolts out of that log and split all our house posts and beams out of them. Long shakes for siding, shingles, almost everything. That first cabin we had there was entirely built out of that one log. I only bought the glass for the windows, some lumber for the floor and some nails and hardware. About ten dollars worth. It was quite a cozy little place too.

After we bought an old stove and a couple of coal oil lamps we had sixty dollars left. Our neighbours were just marvelous. Like you used to find in nearly all them outlaying areas. One family brought us nine sacks of potatoes, just give them to us. Another old lady gave us about two dozen big sealers of sauerkraut. It was an enormous help, sauerkraut and potatoes go a long way (laughs). Another family gave us big batch of oolechans.

After we had our cabin finished I started clearing a bit of land. That was fairly open country there, in a way. It's been logged off and burned off many times. But there was young second growth coming up every where and all the old stumps was still in. This was the type of land that has about forty stumps per acre. Big stumps. At first we didn't have any money for stumping powder so we did it all by hand. We used to go and dig around and dig under the stump and start a fire. Keep a fire burning for a whole week, two weeks sometimes. You've got a half dozen fires burning and you go around chopping off pieces of stump and jambing them under to burn off the roots. Gradually we got about five acres rough cleared. Not all in one year of course. After I got a job and some money, we could afford stumping powder and we blew the last stumps out.

The next spring I was able to sell my land up in the Peace River. Because of the war, grain and cattle prices had gone up somewhat and, more important, there was a market for them. I sold it to the guy who'd been renting it. Got nine hundred dollars for it, spaced out over three years. It wasn't very much but it gave me the start I needed to build up again. That money and most of the money I earned went into building up the new farm. I got into raising angora rabbits then and started making hutches and breeding angoras.

When I got the homestead in the Columbia Valley started and got Hilde settled in I had to find some job. We weren't going to make any money off that place for a while and I was without money to live on. That's when I started to work in logging camps. I worked in many little logging camps along the coast during 1940 and '41 and '42 and even later—until our place started to pay for itself.

CAMP WORK

All the hiring for these camps was out of Vancouver. Things was opening up very slowly in 1940, still like the depression in some ways. The wages hadn't improved much. There were lots of employment offices down on Cordova Street. That wasn't a skid row then, you know. Some of the logging outfits had their own employment offices. Other employment agencies did the hiring for twenty, thirty little camps. There was one really big one then, Black's Logging Employment. They were really hated by the loggers for all the dirty tricks they played. But if you were new and didn't know your way around, Black's was the place to go. Because they had contracts with the most companies and had the most jobs.

I went from office to office every day, to logging agencies and to mining employment offices. If you were there when the work order came in and you looked alright to them, you got the job. If you weren't there, tough luck. Then one day one of these agents says, "They want a bull cook and flunky for DeVeney's camp." Thirty dollars a month and room and board. That was pretty poor wages even in them days. Besides, it was up in Simoon Sound, eighteen dollars fare on the Union (Steamship) boat. But I needed some money bad so I took it.

I went up to Simoon Sound on the next boat going up the coast. It took an endless time. Eventually we got to this one place, just a float wharf and a couple of houses, and they dumped us off there. Old DeVeney came along with a little gas boat and it took another four hours going up the inlet till we got to his camp. There were hundreds of those small outfits scattered along the coast.

I was up in that camp, the first one I been in. DeVeney's wife did the cooking. There was her and DeVeney and only about thirteen, fourteen men in the woods crew. That was a pretty typical size for those small float camps. If the camp was making up a boom to send to the sawmill there'd be some boom men in camp too. They was just there to help out with the boom and after that was finished they'd get their fare back to Vancouver.

This was a haywire bunch of guys. DeVeney, I found out later, had a reputation along the coast as being one of the worst outfits going. He wasn't doing too well and his equipment was all haywire and unsafe. He'd hire guys that couldn't get into other camps; most of them wouldn't have been there if they had a choice. The worst part of it was that some of these little outfits couldn't pay their bills. They'd give you a check when you quit and when you come to town and try to cash that check it'd be no good. Then you had to wait around and hope that the operator would get on his feet enough so that you could cash your check. You'd be broke and running up bills in the mean time.

After about two months up there I'm working around the kitchen and the owner is talking to his wife. They're both half soused—it was a terrible isolated life for a woman. DeVeney says, "I got to get five or six more men to finish off here. Get the boom ready and get it sent down." The raft took all the logs down to Vancouver. His wife says, "What are you going to do? You only got one raft to get ready. You can't bring up a crew just for that." "Oh well," he says. "As soon as I'm finished I'll just let them go." "Then you got to pay their way out," she says. "No, I wouldn't do that. To hell with them. I'll just fire them and that's it. I'm going to fire the rest of them too. I won't need them anyway." And I heard all that.

When the crew came in that night I said, "You guys only going to be here for a week or so more, then he's going to let you go. You got your fare ready?" "That son of a bitch," they say. The next morning they had breakfast and got up and all walked off the job. I walked off with them. DeVeney was stomping around cursing for a while and then he left. Without that boom to send out he was in trouble. Nobody would stay. "We're going to town, we've got enough of this bullshit." That was my first experience in a logging camp and I'd hardly made a penny. I only got about sixty dollars in them two months and thirty-six went for fare.

The next place I worked was for Soderman and that was a very interesting experience. He was a Swede and had a reputation for a first class outfit, one of the best camps along the coast. Also on floats. Sidney, his wife, lived in that camp, too.

I was bull cook and flunky again and she was my boss. I got pretty sick up there with lumbago—that had been coming on since I worked in the mine. Sometimes I could hardly bend my back, and very painful too. But she said, "Hey, don't worry. I'll look after you. You don't need to worry, just rest. Your wages go right on. You're a good boy" (laughs). She used to do a lot of my work bullcooking. I enjoyed working with her very much.

Sidney was known up and down the coast at that time. She'd started out up in the north country when they was putting through the railway to Prince Rupert. Later she run this whore house in Prince Rupert for years. But that was much earlier. She was in her sixties when I knew her, a shrunken up old lady with a straw bonnet on her head. But still fast and quick. I seen once where a logger tried to take her picture and she jumped him and threw the camera in the chuck. She said, "What's the big idea? Why you want to take a picture of an old bag like me? What's the matter with you?" And she hated that man from there on in.

There was signs up in the dining room—"No Talking". The cook said, "Don't talk with these men in the cookhbouse." "Like hell. I'll talk with these men whenever I feel like it," I says. That "no talking" rule was standard in all the camps. Because life was unbearable in camp and the only place the men could bitch was in the dining room. No matter how good the food was, and you never ate better than in them camps, once the wrinkles were out of their stomachs, when they came back from town, they'd start bitching. They'd want hot cakes square instead of round, and stuff like that.

I was supposed to clean up around the camp office too. Sidney had a commissary in there and there was money laying around everywhere, in envelopes and in drawers and everywhere. She says, "You can straighten that up too and if you need a dollar or two just take it. Don't take too much though." "Oh I won't steal nothing." "That's alright. You just take some if you need it," she says. And that was the way many of these camps was run. How to put it? There was a sort of rough but underlying human closeness. Between some people anyway. That is completely lost in the camps today, it doesn't exist at all. Maybe in rare instances, but as a whole I don't think so.

Anyway, my lumbago got so bad that I just couldn't work anymore. It came and went. After four or five years the vertebrae solidified and I didn't have no trouble with it. But during those years that lumbago got so bad that it would knock me right off my feet sometimes. I said, "Sidney, I got to go home and rest." "Okay," she says. "If at any time you need a job you just phone our place in the Grosvenor (Hotel) or wire up. You always got a job here." And she meant it too. But for some reason or another I never got back there.

I worked in a lot of little logging camps over the next few years. I'd be maybe half the year up on the farm with Hilde and close to half the year out in some camp or another. I never stayed more than two, three months in a camp before coming down. Most of the men didn't put in more than three months at a spell. It depended partly on how far up the coast the camp was. Because you had to pay your own fare, which was pretty steep. You got paid one way fare after sixty days.

In them days the camps closed down in summer time; fire season was nearly always in effect by early July. Especially with steam donkeys, there was just too many sparks. They'd maybe have permission to work just early in the morning. But that didn't pay anyway. So the men would just pack up and close her down till early September. The camps would run until Christmas time, that was a pretty standard time to close down for the winter. Some of the big camps operated through the winter but not the small ones. It might be March, even early April till you could get out again to some of these camps. During the year a lot of the small ones would close down for one thing or another. That broke the year up.

The traditional logger went out and made a stake and wanted to be a logger and nothing else. He'd come down to town and blow his stake and go back into the woods. He never gets married and he never has anything to show for all the years of terribly hard dangerous work he did. Some of them eventually get involved with a girl and get married. Even then they don't have what you could call a real family life. But that type of logger was dying out even in my time.

It's true, you do get accustomed to that camp life after a while. That happened to me too. Let's say you been out in camp for three, four months, completely cut off from a normal social life. No women around. When you come out with a stake in your pocket and hit town—something astonishing happens to you. It even happened to me and I'm a comparatively stable individual. You just go off your rocker. Something takes place that's hard to explain. You go on a sort of binge, sort of getting high with the need to socialize with other people. It's that long spell stuck away in camp. I sent my money home and I didn't have much in my pocket when I landed in Vancouver. If I had I might have blown it in just like everybody else. That's all gone today because not many of the logging camps are that isolated anymore. Most of them are now like villages, women and families and everything out there. And that's probably a pretty good thing.

Some of these railway logging camps on the Island already had little villages at their main camp. I worked in one, Elk River Timber, in from the Campbell River. They had over two hundred men in three camps, over a hundred in the main camp. That was the biggest logging camp I ever worked in. A pretty good set-up too. You could get in and out and it was a little more like a normal job. I stayed there for almost four months, the longest I ever stayed. But mainly I worked in a string of small camps. I can't even recall them all.

Logging crews were mainly all grown men. Only the whistle punk would be a pretty young kid just starting out. Whistle punk was a comparatively responsible job, signalling the donkey, he had men's lives in his hands. As soon as possible the whistle punk would try to get a job setting choker. Once guys started setting choker they either stayed at that or got on the loading crew. They usually gave you a chance to learn. The boss said, "Come on, give it a try." If you done half way well you stayed with that job. The fallers were something else again, because they were a closed bunch and I don't know where they got a start. And with high riggers, I can't understand how they caught on to that work. Just kind of tried it out I guess.

Guenther Light came down from the Peace River and managed to bluff his way into falling about that time. He was a neighbour and a close friend of mine up in Peace River. He came down to Vancouver about a year after we did. Light had the nerve to go out into the logging camps as a faller when he had never in his life pulled one of those seven foot falling saws. Oh, he cut down trees in the Peace River and did a bit of logging there. Even I did, logging for one of them two by four tie mills. But them were just matchsticks compared to these huge trees you have here on the coast. It was just completely different.

He goes down to one of them employment agencies and after a week or so gets a chance at falling. "Are you experienced?" they ask him. "Oh sure. I been hand logging for years." He didn't have a clue of what was required of him, and a faller is a part of a team. There were usually three men together at that time, two men on the crosscut saw and a bucker. That was before chain saws came in. The fallers would work from spring boards, six, eight feet off the ground, bouncing around there. Guenther had never even seen a spring board (laughs).

So he comes out to camp where he meets these two other guys. He starts talking to them and right away they know what's up. The next day they go out in the woods and Guenther doesn't know the first thing. But they were pretty good sports. They tried to show him what do do. He lasted two days. By that time they said, "This is impossible. I mean, this just won't do." So he gets sent down to town. Then he went to another outfit and gets sent up to a big camp where somehow he manages to last two weeks before he's fired. From that he was able to pick up enough of falling and working in the woods that he was able to hold down a job in a logging camp. I pulled that bluff myself on some jobs but I still don't know how he managed to get away with it falling.

Some of these fallers made pretty good money doing contract work. That is a mean, destructive system, in my eyes. It's really based on greed. Contract work drives men far beyond the point of endurance. These guys came in every day boasting about how much they cut that day, completely exhausted. A lot of these fallers would only work under contract, they didn't want to work any other way. It burnt a lot of them out, that system. Maybe some days they did twice as much work as anybody would do on a straight wage. Which was hard enough anyway. The other jobs in the woods, like setting choker and yarding crews and everything was on a wage rate, so much per day. They would high ball too but hardly ever like in this contract work. There were a lot of accidents that happened due to that pressure.

I was working up in some small gyppo outfit behind Sechelt when I heard Guenther was getting married. Although I needed the money badly I said, "The hell with it," and went into town to go to his wedding. So you see I was getting that logger's attitude. After that I got a job with a little outfit on Vedder Mountain where I could get home a couple times a week. I been out in the woods and seen all the operations done but I never done any of that work myself. I tried setting choker a short while but I wasn't up to it. Most of the time I was working around the logging camps I was so crippled up with lumbago that I couldn't handle any heavy work. Not so as I could keep up to the pace demanded.

OF THE COLUMBIA VALLEY

Around Columbia Valley there were still family outfits cutting shingle bolts and that sort of thing. They'd cut out trees and lost logs that the big logging companies left behind when they pulled out. That valley has been logged over two, three times. By big railroad outfits and truck loggers and then these little salvage loggers. The first outfits only took the cream, only the best and easiest wood to get—then pulled out. They left a lot of cedar in there. Cedar dropped in price and wasn't profitable to them. So some families around there would go in and cut the cedar up and make shingle bolts and haul them down to some small mill. They made what was then a living wage.

There were people all around the Fraser Valley doing that sort of thing. They worked in camps when there was jobs. But when there wasn't or when they felt like working on their own they worked around home in the hills. Usually they had some sort of little stump ranch. That was true of all the area back of Cultus Lake and Rosedale and throughout that whole bench country around the Valley. Back up of Hatzic and Mission and Agassiz and all through there. They were taking out logs from pockets on the side hills that the timber companies left behind, and turned it into money. Not much, but enough. So that's where many young guys got their start. They helped their dad or relatives or neighbour doing this salvage logging. Getting the feel of how to handle the saws and axes and chains and stuff.

For a couple of winters Hilde and me did that kind of thing too, right off our homestead. There was a fairly good market for poles and stakes. They used a lot of poles in the hop yards, and a different size as bean poles and still a different size for raspberries and who knows what else. I took a contract for 120,000 bean poles once. Hilde and I went out and found these high stumps, cedar stumps six, eight, ten feet high, still standing from twenty years before. Usually they're scorched on the outside because fire goes through this logged over land time and again.

You cut these cedar snags down and a few inches inside it's still beautiful old growth cedar. It splits up very easy. At first we pulled the saw by hand, a long two man crosscut saw. Then one of our neighbours lent us a (gas driven) drag saw They never used drag saws in the woods much because the thing's too heavy and clumsy. Lifting it over big logs, up side hills and swamps and thick bush, no. It wasn't no good for logging but for bucking-up in that logged off area we were working in a drag saw helped a lot.

Hilde and I cut down these cedar snags and bucked them into blocks. We made a shed and we'd stand there in the pouring rain in February, March, and April splitting the blocks into poles. It was a delightful job because that cedar runs so freely from your hand. Almost no effort at all. We didn't do too badly. We made about six or seven dollars a day. It all helped.

We also made cedar fence posts, thousands of them, and hauled them out to the road. Cedar posts were in demand because they didn't rot. Now all fence posts are made from jack pine shipped from up country. We cut fire wood for sale a couple of years too. I sold it down in Chilliwack but the transport costs were too high to make anything.

That Columbia Valley was originally settled from the American side. They'd come in from the railway at Maple Falls (Washington) in the 1880's and many of the original families was still there. There was no road in from the Fraser Valley until long after. They cleared their land entirely by hand, some fairly big acreages too. Over a hundred acres. It must have been a fantastic amount of work, much harder than in the Peace River. That bench country is quite rocky and it's nowhere near as fertile as the Fraser Valley. For a fact, it's questionable whether it's really suitable as a farming area. That's why it never went ahead, why those farms been in there so long and never made much head way.

In some ways that community in the Columbia Valley was

very different from what I experienced homesteading in the Peace River. Up in the Peace River we were all newcomers, with all sorts of different backgrounds, from all over the world. We were building up our district fresh, right in front of our eyes. And we were very committed to progress and not standing still. But in the Columbia Valley most of those families been there a couple of generations. They were mostly all intermarried and related in one way or another. Mostly all Yugoslav, originally. They were a easy going but lively bunch. It was a kind of a hillbilly community. That may not be the right word, because I don't mean that as an insult in any way.

What I appreciated very much was their down-to-earthness. You could sit down with an old lady and discuss sex, or the latest operation or any other problem anybody had. Or anything else that was part of their lives. All in a completely natural way. There wasn't any community organization like we had in the Peace River but there was quite a bit of social activity through house parties. Even no church ever got much of a foothold there. Although they didn't have the slightest interest in books or what you might call cultural things, they were otherwise full of spark and vitality.

I got to know most of their kids pretty well. They were an astonishingly gifted lot. Hardly any education, missed much of the school year the few years when they did go. But they had a patience and a sense that was amazing. I seen these kids take a generator apart. Didn't know the first thing about how a generator runs. They'd fix it, put it back together again, put it in and make it work. That, to me, is damn near a miracle. I wouldn't dare try something like that.

In the same way they would take a whole motor apart, to grind the valves let's say. They had endless time and patience. If it didn't work the first time, well, they took it apart and put it together again until it did work. It didn't matter if they didn't get the motor fixed today. If it was fixed tomorrow or the day after, or the day after that, that was just as good. The rest of us always want to get things done in a hurry. It's a totally different attitude. And I really enjoyed that more relaxed way of doing things.

There were ten, twelve kids in each family. The girls, when they were fourteen or fifteen years old, got pregnant and then got married. Hardly any of them ever got left stranded. The young couple would live with one of the parent's families and the boy would work around the farm. Maybe he would work out part of the year. And they all got by. Generally they seemed contented.

They were awfully set in their ways when it came to farming. When I had some land cleared I plowed lime into my new pasture and planted alfalfa. I used mashed up rabbit pellets as manure, and I got some tremendously heavy alfalfa crops off my five acres. I thought I could stimulate some of the others in the Valley to go for alfalfa because they all had cattle. But they weren't interested. They stayed with their own tried ways of doing things. They raised a lot of potatoes and cabbages. Grass pasture for their cows. Most of them shipped a little milk out every day. But they always managed to get by in fair comfort.

While I was out in the camps Hilde looked after the farm and took care of the rabbits. We'd gotten into raising Angoras for wool. I was back every few months and that's when we did the building around the place. With rabbits there's not much problem increasing the stock. You just have to make sure you breed right, to keep their breeding records straight. You tatoo their ears and work out what you think will be the best breeding combination from going through their production records. Clipped and plucked them and sent our wool to the States. I sold breeding stock to almost every state in the U.S. and every province in Canada.

There was a whole group of us around the Fraser Valley and I helped set up a breeders and producers coop for angoras. There was a good price for angora wool and we made fairly good money. After '43 I stayed out of the logging camps. I had about four hundred rabbits and that was a full time job. You feed them and water them and clean out their hutches. All by hand, all in the most primitive way, with buckets and dippers. You have to brush them pretty regular. And I still grew quite a bit of the feed for them too.

The angora business was sound for about three years. But starting about 1946 or 1947, shipments of angora wool came in from Europe and Japan. The market was flooded and collapsed. Top grade, extra long, plucked angora wool dropped from eighteen dollars a pound to around four dollars a pound. Lower grades that make up most of the wool you get, they were less than half that. We couldn't begin to produce it for that. The company that we sold to cancelled the order for the wool I'd already shipped. I had sixteen hundred dollars outstanding, which I never got. The angora business was finished.

We hung on for another year or so, raising some pigs and calves. I had a beautiful little herd of goats. They are wonderful animals for that logged-off scrub country. They're natural browsers and they do very well on that kind of land. We drank goat milk and made cheese and raised some terrific pigs and calves on the milk. But you couldn't give goat milk away and nobody wanted goats. Partly we lived on the little money we had saved up.

Anyway, we couldn't make a living off the place anymore. And I didn't want to go out to camps again. There was a communal farm in the process of getting organized down in the Fraser Valley and some of the people in it approached me to see if I'd be interested in joining. That's what we decided to do. That must have been very early in the spring of 1949.

I didn't sell our place in the Columbia Valley all at once. I sold it in three blocks over a time. I got, on an average, about thirty dollars an acre. Even less for the uncleared land. Now that same land is two thousand an acre at least, without a lick of work done on it. It's very desirable land now. I first sold off the five acres cleared and the house and buildings and we moved down to that communal farm at Mud Bay in the Serpentine Valley, near Cloverdale.

From Communal Farm
To Chicken Ranch

A NEW HOME

The whole idea of being in a communal farm appealed to me. But it was a poorly financed and poorly laid out venture. The land was very costly and the payments were just murder. The land was terribly run down. Some of it was flooded and to get it into cultivation was costly and slow. It was completely infested with weeds and crab grass and couch grass. That land has to be drained almost continually or it's useless. The drains were all broken down and plugged. Water washed down off the ridge on to the flats and just sat there. Putting in a big drainage ditch cost us two thousand dollars, an enormous amount of money to us. And that was just one of the things that had to be repaired.

We always had trouble with finances and with getting a market for what we produced. For instance, one crop we had at the end of our first season was twenty-two acres of pumpkins. Fine ones, too. I think we came out something like fifteen dollars to the good on them Our twenty acres of potatoes was just as bad. We did a little better on some of the other crops but there was over-production in all lines and there was just no price paid for them at all. Instead of getting ahead of the game we were always a little behind.

One part of it was that we always had our stuff ready just a bit too late, when the market was already glutted. You harvest just a few weeks too late and you take a tremendous loss in that market garden line. You get a little behind with planting or weeding and each phase adds on. You wind up missing whatever market there is. Then we got into growing grass seed.Growing the seed for people to plant lawns with (laughs). That could have been a very good move because the price was high. We had the right land and there wasn't much competition.

There were five families living in that communal farm. About a dozen adults and maybe ten kids, regularly. There was our master farmer, a retired farmer that come out from Saskatchewan, who was supposed to be a sort of advisor. Some of the others had some kind of farm background but never had anything to do with farming since they were kids. One of the frictions was between them and this master farmer. He sort of felt paternal, that farming decisions should come from him. He was a wonderful person, very generous and very willing and he kicked in some of his own money. But that wasn't the idea. The group wanted to participate in every decision. There developed a continual friction—even when his ideas were absolutely, completely correct.

These people, as inspired as they were, most of their lives had been involved in planning and not in real physical work. They would sit down every night, having coffee till eleven or twelve o'clock, and plan what to do next day or next year or God knows what. I think they found fulfillment in that. Gradually they learned and got to realize how you have to work. If we'd had enough time I think the farm would have come along alright. But it takes quite a while before you get into the habit of putting in a full day's work. They wouldn't show up till about ten o'clock next morning. Then there'd be a long lunch hour. And we were in a pressing need, a desperate need, to be out working on the land. To get things fixed up and producing. I chewed my fingernails off trying to get at it and they were piddling away. And that caused some friction.

We only had one tractor and very little equipment. Actually we didn't need all that much and I think we would have got what we needed if we could have hung on. There was four, sometimes five, men working in the fields on the average.

The women did come out and help in the fields a bit but not too often. You only needed extra help at certain times. We never had any animals that they could have worked with.

There was so much that overlapped that the women never really got into the farming end. But it's quite true, there was never any real attempt made to get the women involved in the productive side of the set up. There were children to take care of and cooking and there wasn't much liberation of women from housework. Because I don't think any of us men every done much of it. It might have been more rewarding all the way around if we'd mixed the work, a little bit anyway. We was actually quite radical, but that sort of thing didn't occur to us. Or if it did we settled into the old pattern pretty quick.

Along with this struggle to get the land into production and worrying about how we were going to meet the payments, we had to put up housing for all of us. We put up four buildings with two apartments in each one. One of them was a kind of kindergarten. We built a big community kitchen and dining room. That was very good, to my mind, but it created additional problems as time went on. Each family cooking for itself is a very ingrained habit, you know, and it's hard for most people to get over it very easily. Two of the women had some university training in home economics or nutrition or something and they figured they should sort of direct the kitchen. That didn't work at all.

Sharing out the income from that farm wasn't a source of friction. Because there was never any. No surplus anyway. Most of your needs was taken care of. That all came out of operating funds. It was just for personal items like clothing and luxuries and books that you needed money. Regardless of what you put into that farm or how long you worked, each couple was supposed to get so much money as their own each month. A percentage of the surplus. That was the way it was supposed to work if we'd ever had any surplus to distribute. There was a separate fund for the children.

The most marvelous thing was the children, the way they grew up together. At least I enjoyed that enormously. I always thought it did them a world of good to grow up where they learned to get on with other children. Where they had to learn to get on with others and to slowly appreciate the needs and qualities of others. The kids there were anywhere from babies to ten years old. We come to the agreement that everybody was going to take a certain degree of responsibility for these kids. Not just the parents themselves. Of course there was no thought of replacing the family or anything like that (laughs).

But we as a group attempted to apply progressive methods of raising children. I thought that was very good. But our master farmer, he must have been in his late sixties, he was absolutely horrified at the lack of discipline among the children. He was a socialist to the very core. He read everything there was to read about socialism and he was willing and committed. But he just couldn't change his attitude. He always felt there had to be more discipline.

Watson Thomson was the main organizer of that farm. He was an advisor to the first C.C.F. government in Saskatchewan for a while. An outstanding person, very dynamic in a gentle way. Most of us respected him and his views very deeply. I still got some of his books about "the struggle for power" and on "communal life" around here somewhere.

Our group could carry on the second year only because Watson Thomson sold his house and loaned us the money and went back to U.B.C. to earn some money teaching. A couple of other men got part time jobs and that kept our heads above water for a while. We had twenty acres of land on Panorama ridge, on a bench overlooking the Serpentine Valley. Finally we sold some house lots on that ridge, a beautiful view. That helped quite a bit because them lots sold for two thousand dollars each, which we thought was just fantastic money. Half acre and acre lots. Now they're worth at least ten times as much. Anyway, that's how we hung on.

Everybody on the farm was intelligent enough and willing enough. If we hadn't started on such an expensive place and at that particular time I think we would have made it. One could be quite happy in a life like that. Mind you, not every individual fits into that kind of life. I read where they have their share of problems in the Kibbutz too. It depends on a great many different factors. Depends upon the personalities involved, how each group fits together, how they enjoy each other's company. The secret is to learn to live with people who you don't particularly enjoy. And I think people can accomplish that. It's not as hard as we are always told and think. There are some differences which probably cannot be bridged. But once you determine to get along you soon discover there are always some bases of agreement or appreciation. Children are an enormous help in that regard. So that was the adventure there for me.

In the end we left. We were there not quite two years. That farm couldn't carry on as it was, financially it was finished. I sold the land that was left on our place in the Columbia Valley and got about four hundred dollars. After endless looking I found this place where we are now, outside of Langley, and I rented it.

WORKING OUT AND CHICKEN RANCHING

The place we rented wasn't like it is today. It was four acres of overgrown meadow with a little shack in a terrible state of neglect and a couple of old sheds in the back that was supposed to be barns. I still had a few head of cattle and a few goats and some rabbits. We moved them down to this place and tried to make some sort of a living. I took my four hundred dollars and put a downpayment on that place.

I got a bank loan and went into raising chickens. You know them old stories, "People always have to eat, and they always are gonna want eggs. So this has gotta be a sound as rock investment." It only took about a year before I got knocked out of the chicken business. I should have known because there were lots of chicken houses around here standing empty, falling down. But I was determined to hang on to this place and I stayed with it. So I had to go out to work and I wound up back in the camps.

Kitimat was the first construction camp I been in. I remember when I stepped off the boat it was snowing, I was down in the dumps, and that's the way I remember it. There was always men streaming in and out of that place. I went up there two times, stayed quite a while and made some pretty big money. We paid off a good chunk of the farm and got back into raising chickens from the stake I made at Kitimat. But it was one of the most empty, terribly empty times in my life.

After nine months I came home and said, "I'm never going out again." And I was as certain as anything that I meant it But we had very little money coming in, and a few months later I was up in the Bridge River in another construction camp. That is lovely country up there and I liked it better than Kitimat. But it was still camp life. The last time I went out was to a pulp mill near Campbell River, about 1955. When I came out of there we had the farm almost paid off and the chickens was bringing in some money. From then on I stayed home. I still had to take jobs to get us through. But they were all jobs in the Fraser Valley and I could at least get home at night and live something like a normal life.

In '55 and '56 I had a job on the green chain in Brown's, a broken down old sawmill down near Patullo Bridge. One of the oldest in B.C. at that time. I worked for five months on the night shift. Then it sold out to an American outfit and closed up and we was all laid off. I went to the Unemployment Office and one of the guys there says, "Why don't you try Woodlands School? They're always looking for people." I always been interested in children in one way or another and this Woodlands School was for severely retarded children. So I went down. The chief there says to me, "This is just what you want. You'll have to be a father and a mother to these kids." Which was a ridiculous exaggeration. But I took the job and the eleven years I worked there was one of the most rewarding episodes of my life.

I worked on the spastic ward at first, which had children who was very responsive and bright. Very sad, too, to see these personalities trapped inside bodies that don't work. Well yes, frankly, you got a little callous after a while. Maybe that's not the right word. You get used to it so it doesn't bother you. That is absolutely necessary.

I went back to Woodlands for visits for years after I left. Even after six years, if I went back to the wards where I worked, all the kids still knew me. But if I go back now, it's a very difficult affair for me. When you're working there you soon lose all tendency to be upset by physical appearances. You get used to it, it doesn't mean anything to you. Then you can get to the real personality within that physical shell. But when I go in now I see all these twisted bodies. It is quite difficult for me to find the easy natural way with them right away.

Many patients had four, five things wrong with them. They may be retarded and have a biff, be paralyzed from the waist down and are somewhat spastic or epileptic on top of it. Very few had only one thing physically wrong. But the courage of some of them; especially the spastics, is really inspiring to see. How they struggle on. One kid made a shawl for me for Christmas on a special weaving frame. Just to get his arm and hand to make one strand took him minutes of determined concentration. It took him six months to make that shawl. You wouldn't think that a human being would have the patience and persistence to do that. But they do. They dig down to something that most of us never even know exists within us, till life really demands it of us.

We had a routine. There'd be dressing and undressing and feeding and cleaning up the patients and keeping them occupied during the day. Forty to fifty in a ward. Some days would be bath day. Even that is a job which you can either make enjoyable and pleasant for the patient or you can make it into a rush routine. That depends completely on the people you work with and the response of the patients. There are difficult days. But you come to accept that and know that tomorrow or the day after will be a better day. As long as there isn't too much friction between the head nurse and the staff under her. That's often the main problem in these big institutions, there's a lot of internal friction between the staff.

After a few years I took a special course at U.B.C. in training retarded children. I did that for two winters and even took off work one summer to complete the course. It wasn't so much teaching them as keeping the kids happily occupied. I developed my own program on the ward, against much resistance from some old line staff. But from year to year Woodlands improved. The new chief who came in had a big part in changing it. Gradually even the old timers on the ward realized that their jobs depended on going along with those improvement projects. So they stopped sabotaging them.

One experience I had—there were thousands of them—was with a boy about eleven years old. The rest of the staff really disliked him because he had no speech but would get around everywhere on the ward and pick up things and hide them. "Oh, he steals, steals everything," they said. He was always in trouble. Patients had no personal belongings whatever, nothing that belonged to them alone. I could see that there was a need for him to have something of his own. So after I opened my playroom I let him look after the toys and put them away. That kid got so that he could read my mind, so that even before I said that I wanted something done, he did it. We had a marvelous relationship.

This went on for about three years. Then one summer I went on vacation. When I came back he had taken on the care of an elderly patient on the ward. Over night he dropped the need to hang around me. At first I was almost hurt about it. Then I realized that this was the very thing that I wanted to happen. Because he could now transfer his affections to someone else and he got along very well from then on. But then there were other incidents too that were extremely tragic.

My wages paid our living expenses and whatever we made from the farm we plowed back into it again. The wages were pitiful low at first. I started out at about a hundred and ninety dollars a month in 1956. The janitors were the first to get unionized. For a while they got more money than the custodial staff. That's what a good union will do. Then the Government Employees Association started to get a little active. I supported it but I wasn't active organizing. But we finally started to make contracts that were reasonable. I worked at Woodlands until 1967 and on my sixtieth birthday I had to retire. Compulsory retirement at sixty. The farm was doing pretty well and I had a bit of a pension so I didn't mind too much. But we still had to have an income.

Although Hilde and me took it a bit easier, raising chickens was a full time job. We used to raise specialty birds, like small fryers and capons or a batch of those large meat roosters. About '62 or '63 they came out with a new type of bird with improved genetics. These birds put on weight at an enormous rate and mature very early. They're ready in nine weeks after you get the chicks from the hatchery. They're broad chested fryers with a lot of meat on them and with a fantastic feed to meat ratio. For a few years you could do very well with the right birds and the right feed schedules. You could make a decent living at it.

So right away there's a rush into the chicken business. It's not too long before the prices start to drop and the small producer was in trouble again. You got to build big enough so per unit costs is small. That is the big pressure behind it all. You make so little per unit that you got to be big. That pressure is in all areas of agriculture just as much as anywhere else. Maybe even worse in agriculture. Raising chickens nowadays—they're not like animals at all anymore. It's not like farming anymore. It's like being a businessman and running a factory. And I don't like that. But if you don't keep up with these trends you're pushed out.

We done what we could in forming the B.C. Chicken Marketing Board. That helped stop take-over of the chicken business by the big feed companies and a few big operators. It was a terrific struggle at the time. It was almost a miracle to me that we convinced the majority of the people raising chickens that they should give over some direction of production to a market board. Then we had to argue with the Social Credit government to allow us to set up a Marketing Board. They only allowed us that vote because they thought we would lose.

But just as we were organizing the bottom dropped out of the chicken market. Even a middle sized producer could lose everything in two or three batches of birds. All that it took was that the prices dropped maybe two cents below the cost of production. The consumers didn't even notice it. But it meant life and death to us. So even the free enterprizers was desperate and voted for the Marketing Board.

Many of the people we had to convince were

dyed-in-the-wool free enterprizers. You know, "This is a free country. We must have the right to produce whatever we like, whenever we like, and sell it at whatever we want to." A market board has the tendency to stabilize the industry. It takes the extremes out of the market, it takes the speculation out of it. The true free enterprizer is basically a speculator. He doesn't want a stable market. He doesn't want the bust but he wants to be in on the boom (laughs). He always believes that if everyone minded their own business it would be boom times all year, every year. He doesn't accept that it doesn't work out like that (laughs).

I always built up on what cash I had. I didn't use credit except to get the farm. Today you could never get a start that way; with small scale production you'd never even earn production costs. Today the small guy that wants to get into farming is frozen right out. That sort of building up from scratch is just part of history now. There's still a lot of baloney that you can still make it with hard work and the sweat of your brow and all that. But most of these guys starting out small now will always just be working for the bank—working and taking the risks.

The banks are always for lending the small farmer money when times are good. But as soon as there's the least difficulty they clamp right down and you're left sitting high and dry. A lot of people lost their places by not being able to make the payments on their loans. That's no different than it's ever been. I seen that too often.

So that's about where we are today.

Reflections

June 1972

I have one regret; that I haven't participated in political and municipal activities more. When I left Woodlands I thought I would become more active in the Coop and in municipal affairs. But somehow, due to the life I've become used to, I couldn't seem to get away from running the farm.

I'm a member of the N.D.P. but just attending meetings and putting in my two cents worth. Sometimes I think that even now it's not too late to do something more active. It might be a good thing for me but I'm not sure if it's a good thing for any movement to be cluttered up with a great many old people in control.

But I realize that people are what's needed. What is needed is active members, even more than directors and organizers. There are very few people in organizations who will speak up from the floor. If you do speak up you soon get elected to some position or other and that makes the floor even less of a participant. I've come to realize that one does play a role, and maybe an important role, in being just a regular attender. One who speaks up when something comes along that you know something about. That is what I should have been doing more of, when it was possible. Going to Council meetings and community meetings and political meetings. Often I was just too tired, or it rained or it snowed or one thing or another (laughs). And I regret that. I had every intention to get more involved in the community in general.

Things have changed some since we finished the story. Hilde and me are getting on and running the farm got to be a bit too much for me on my own. A young couple were helping me run it. They very much wanted to get into farming but didn't see where they'd have a chance to start. Two years ago we decided to sell off to them. I wanted to pass on the farm to somebody that really wanted to farm, rather than just selling at the highest price I could get and maybe having some speculator get hold of it. They got a pretty good deal because I'm carrying most of the mortgage myself and the Farm Credit Union picked up the rest.

We've got an arrangement where Hilde and me can stay on the farm in this mobile home we set up in the corner. And I help around the place, which gives me just enough to do to stay active. Doing no work at all would be just horrible. So it is a good arrangement both ways. I started having some trouble with my heart and the wet winters hit me something awful. Getting old is terrible, but I guess it comes to all of us.

Hilde and me try to get away for a trip once a year. We been to Hawaii and we been to West Germany twice. The first time I hadn't been back in over forty years. We think we've got a consumer society here, where you got the choice of fifteen brands of the same toilet paper and endless advertising and competing. Well, in West Germany they got us beat by a mile. The most frenzied consumer society you ever seen. Where the money comes from I don't know.

We been to East Germany too and I just got back from a trip to Poland, the part where I grew up (former German territory south of Breslau). I only now come to realize how big the differences can be between socialist countries. To my mind there are still a lot of restrictions and bureaucracy in East Germany. Too many decisions coming from the top. Although there are a lot of complaints it seems the younger people there are mainly convinced that they got basically a healthy and sensible system, without the unemployment and fears we got. They're doing miracles with land we wouldn't even think of farming. Big "cooperative" farms that use the most modern machinery and methods on acreages as big as what you see on some prairie wheat farms

On the other hand I been astounded by Poland. True enough, I seen just one part of it. But it seemed very backward. All small peasant farms and very poor. I seen one tractor in a four hour drive. Most were still working with one horse. You can believe it or not but they were still cutting their hay with scythes. What amazed me most of all was the strength of the church. In Poland it wasn't just supported by old people. In the villages we been in you'd see almost everybody going to church—children, young families and older people.

Last year we made a short trip to Cuba. Went on a charter with one of our old neighbours from the Peace River. We spent a lot of time on the beaches but I made some trips around the farming districts too. And that was all different again. It's hard to say, but they seem to be really determined and proud of what they accomplished. In agriculture they are really going ahead. There's one thing that we found in all those socialist countries that we visited. There is a great stress on peace, despite what we are always told.

Now I been a socialist since I first came to Vancouver in the thirties. But these last few years have given me, I think, a greater understanding of the basic directions in our society. They been a reminder. I always hoped that if you cannot do away with the stupid and destructive things in our system in my own lifetime at least you could expect a gradual improvement. I was naive enough to believe that the progress we made could never be wiped out. The security we got in old age pensions, unemployment insurance, health care and so on. But now I am greatly worried that both inflation and the new government in B.C., and in Ottawa too, will take it away, bit by bit, step by step.

And it's not just the government alone, it's people behind them. Not just big business either. People that got a house and made some money on increased land value and right away they feel that it's due to a good system that rewards them fairly. In fact it is just speculative luck and in no way a reward for their labour. All that it means is that somebody coming along later is going to have to pay that increased price and find it almost impossible to do it. All that it takes is that some people have to have a few dollars invested and things get a bit tough and right away they're screaming, "We got to protect the free enterprize system that built all this," and so on.

What I resent most is that whatever I got now came from the inflated value of the farm and that all the years of my hard work provided us with almost no security. But I think I enjoyed most of my life, even with all the struggle. Maybe because of it sometimes.

Mud Bay communal farm, Koeppen and other residents, 1951.

Appendix I
Pages From a Homestead Diary

COMMENTS 50 YEARS LATER

What you got to realize is that I was a very young man, that I was only twenty years old, when this diary starts. During those four years I was only gradually becoming a farmer and becoming Canadianized. People are going to find some of it pretty high flown, even sort of conceited in places (laughs). For a fact, some of it strikes me as pretty humourous when I read it now. Especially where I'm writing about how with work anybody can make a pleasant and comfortable life for himself up there. But I think we should leave that because that's what I actually wrote then. I just hope that people reading the whole story get some idea that my outlook has matured some since I wrote this diary.

Another thing. You got to remember that the Peace River country was really the last homesteading area in Canada. It wasn't really typical of more established farming areas. The terribly primitive conditions we had when we were building up were kind of outdated on the prairies by that time.

Actually—and it's not too clear in the diary—I didn't even start grain farming for myself until I got married. Up till then I cleared land, worked out and was getting together my livestock. I rented out my broken land to Scriba on a share basis. He got two-thirds and I got one-third of the grain from my land delivered to the elevator. That was a standard deal for that kind of arrangement. It was only when I got married that I started grain farming on my own. By that time I had my four horse outfit. That made you a real farmer then. That's when I started to become a real producer and got more tied to market conditions.

One thing I should mention—because it may look kind of

strange to anybody who homesteaded in different kind of country—how it was possible to get almost thirty acres cleared by hand in one year. Others managed that too. This was fairly open parkland. On my homestead there were big natural openings, patches of maybe two, three acres where you only had to clear out a few bluffs (of trees). I'd cut them out and then clear to link up these openings. And I worked like a wild man during the first year.

Not all the Peace River country was like that though. In fact on the way from Wanham you passed stretches of heavy bushland where it would have been near impossible to clear any acreage by hand.

What doesn't come across in the diary, and what we only gradually came to realize, was that the real struggle was not with nature. That too, but that we could handle. I only slowly come to recognize that we could quite successfully build up our farms but that we were still completely manipulated by forces that we had absolutely no control over. That the real struggle was with human, economic forces.

(Ebe Koeppen, July 1977)*

*The present version comprises some two-thirds of Ebe Koeppen's original homestead diary covering November 1928 to July 1932. I have translated from the original German. Deletions were mainly of passages involving philosophizing and general pep talks written by the diarist to himself. We believe that enough such material has been retained here to provide a feel for those facets of Koeppen's life and emotions during his bachelor homestead years. Virtually all entries dealing with day-to-day events on the homestead have been retained.

The diary is fragmentary both in time and topic, with much left unsaid or taken for granted. It contains many provocative, sometimes humourous, internal contradictions. Its most serious limitation is that it deals only with the initial years of starting out and does not document the more rounded phase of homesteading which developed after marriage. Despite these limitations I find the diary a frank and valuable addition to the whole story. It records a realistically less rosy and more fractious picture than the more summary accounts. (RK)

PEACE RIVER DIARY

1928

November 1928. The small loghouse is finished now. Despite mosquitoes and much strife. I'm so inexperienced and unpractical, but still don't like to be advised on everything. The loghouse is comfortable but naturally very primitive. Only some 3 by 4.5 meters. There is a drizzle of dirt from the ceiling, which consists only of logs covered with sod and earth. The floor is terribly rough. Only split poplar that never split straight. We have two small windows and an airtight—a one hole tin stove to cook and heat with. But warm; it gets too warm very quickly.....

I don't rightly know how I'll eventually get the diary back into running account. I'd like to hold on to all the impressions and experiences. How we first saw Heart Valley was like this.

(*In June 1928*) Well from Edmonton we got to Wanham on the railway. A long trip. From Wanham to Heart Valley mainly on foot, on the way we got a few rides. Hans said it was too far from the railway. First, 12 miles to the nearest tiny story and the post office, from there another 4 miles to Fischer and Scriba, then another two miles. People could understand our broken English to some extent and they were all very friendly. The earth looks black and rich and the young seed appeared fabulous. Not everything was sown yet.

Anyway, we went from the store past Michell's, where a very nice woman gave us coffee and biscuits. Then for a long stretch there was nothing. One had to open wire fences and the trail wandered through the open places. Actually the trail is only two tracks ground out by wagon wheels. Everything is open bushland. It is what they call "parkland" here.

We came to a slough. Somebody had driven into it with four horses, which stood there trying to drink with the bits in their mouths. The guy himself stood on a home-made "stoneboat"—two runners made of logs with boards nailed across. On it he had a large wooden barrel, which he was filling full of water with a pail. The horses standing in front of him drank and naturally dropped manure, as all animals usually do when they drink. The man placidly scooped the water into the barrel. Hans and I stood there astounded. It was Fischer, who took us to his cabin. He offered to show us the two best remaining homestead parcels here if we would help him. He is breaking new land, with horses that are half wild and which had some terrible open sores on the shoulders. We did that three days....

(Fischer shows them the homesteads they finally pre-empt but initially they decide to look at another block on the Peace River. An extended description of the trek to the Peace River and rafting the previous June. Also some comments on working on the railroad. The following diary entries return to on-going accounts of establishing the homestead. The first diary entry ends.)

Everything is in harmony with Hans again. I'm happy about that. All the continual dissension, and the many frictions tired me out. Now each of us works on his own place, cooks for himself and we only spend the evenings together. It's pleasant to sit by our coal oil lamps in the cosy warm room. We have made ourselves comfortable already. How much farther ahead am I than those without a place of their own who have to use up their earnings to get through the winter.

November 1928. The water laid us low after a short while. Unboiled, it works like a purgative. Well, it comes of course from some flat open sloughs, with plenty of contented living matter. Mosquitoe larvae? At least 10 to 20 times a day I had to run out and quickly drop my pants. My stomach's continually rumbling and grumbling. An agitated protest against the water. We don't have any potatoes either so the stomach gets loaded down with soft, bulkless foods. Stomach ache and weakness. The work (clearing land) is hard and sometimes I drag myself out to work. The axe doesn't ring anymore. The strokes are only dull and weak. Sad days. From now I'll drink only boiled water. Tomorrow we want to get ice with a wagon. It's supposed to be very good water. We have to borrow horses and wagon from Fischer and drive five miles to Pearson dugout. Today we also got potatoes and a lot of deer meat. Tonight we have goulash with potatoes and noodles, and afterwards compote.

Beginning of winter, November 1928. I don't know the date. As we got up in the morning to go for ice, snow lay on the ground. Happy as a child I ran out and bathed in the snow. Water, beautiful good water. With pleasure I carried one pail of snow after another in to melt it. A real bath—how wonderful. How long did I have to save every cup of water, and now no more.

I guess that land clearing won't be possible but there is plenty else yet to do.

Beginning December. Today it was sunny, a winter beauty such as in early March at home. Dry snow and dry cold, minus 30 centigrade. It is possible to do some clearing in this dry snow.

December 1928. Today I went out for the first time as a trapper and busily laid my traps. It is hard work in this grim cold, to climb through the forest, over fallen trees and roots. If I touch the iron of the traps with my bare hand the skin sticks to it immediately. Probably a lot of experience and an iron nature are required for this work. Down in the valley, cut almost a mile into the flatland by a creek, it is some 10 degrees colder. And that is where the weasles live. But there aren't so many of them. Got a very bad letter from Kurt.....

December 29. Christmas lies behind us. The first in this land. We had a Christmas dinner—roasted two chickens. Some of the older settlers have cows, chickens and pigs and let us work for what they can spare. We even had a Christmas tree and that put us in a Christmas mood. Thanks to the incomparable kindness of some of the English settlers we were supplied with cake, apples and nuts. How these people here treat us young bachelors—with an open, natural generosity.

Everyone received packages and letters, except me. Only a card from a new Canadian friend I met in Rosebud. It was very bitter for me, especially as I didn't know anything about mother's health.

December 1928. I work now for Schrieber, a German who has been in Canada for four years. I will receive $30 in value for a month's work—he will break some of my cleared land with his tractor.....

I was angry when I came home at Christmas. Hans had scattered hay for the horses in front of the house and the horses had dropped their manure everywhere around the door and windows. And in the house—horrible, a pig pen. Everything dirty and unbelievably grimy. It was so coated in dirt that I couldn't stay in my own house, and went over to neighbour Fischer, where we were for Christmas. No matter how difficult it is, I must live alone by spring.

Apart from that, Hans is friendly. He's already bought horses, which was a mistake from a practical standpoint. They give him much pleasure. But this passion takes a lot of time and money.

1929

By January 6, 1929. (Ebe sends to Germany to have the remainder of his personal belongings that he can use sent to Peace River. The immigrant's steamer trunk, with all its implications of permanence.)

January 7. Back to the work place (*clearing land*). Hans' horses stood along the way, pawing in the snow with their forelegs and eating grass. A cow with her calf crossed my path. A singular picture. The guy from Berlin, Licht, took a good photo of my house. Now to work.

January 1929. A very sad point. I have never lived such a terrible, uncomfortable life. Eating is so primitive. Without potatoes, without butter, oats three times a day, rice and beans. Dreary. I have never been so dirty. The towel hasn't been washed in months. God, how dirty we are.

Schreiber, the German farmer, has had the same underwear on for two months. And he hasn't bathed yet. Still, well shaved and courteous. A man who is a pious Christian? Continual, fervent praying, but with overweaning egoism, not with the slightest Christian attitude. The man himself suffers greatly under the indescribable comfortlessness of his life. Only holds on with iron will. I was to continue working for him for four months, but it's impossible.....

Such people go forward, ignoring all else in life. There are many like that here. But the result: despite all energy, after two to three years they are absolutely incapable of holding on longer. Every day for them is already a torture. It is so easy to make a good life here, but they can't. Always claiming, "Well, if we had money then we could live comfortably." Apparently they expect to buy happiness later? Poor bachelors. Already too apathetic to cook. Every day the same feed. It's not possible to feel content in such conditions. Often these questions arise in talk. I do not write home about these things. The staggering drearyness of such existence is too difficult to make understandable.

January 1929. Received a long, detailed letter from Kurt. His mother died on the 5.8.1928. I'm astounded how distant I am from these happenings. They hardly make any impression on me. Of course I only knew her slightly. It is as if these secondary people had already long gone out of my life. Those that still live with me are mother, Kurt, Kriesel, Ruth and Klaus. Is Ruth disappearing as well? Herold's are as if already dead and so Hendrick's.....

(*A long roster of his former friends and relations in Germany follows.*)

I live more in the future than in the present. Daydreaming?—still because of it I live more happily and peacefully in this present. Sometimes I'm gripped by a drive for novelty, sometimes the desire to be a vagabond. Still life on the homestead always requires something new to do, new work, new problems. The work is so hard and taxing, sleep comes quickly. If I only could round up a few hundred dollars. That would make so many things easier.

January 20. Hans shot a moose on his homestead after a

wild hunt on horseback. An indescribable piece of luck. Our larder is now supplied for the winter with meat. My resources are now almost run out. I don't have a cent. It is becoming an unbearable life. In the icy winter cold—minus forty degrees celsius—we skinned the booty. Everywhere blood and great lumps of flesh. We were completely numb with the cold. A wild picture.

Now life shows us its hardness. Without anything, without a board, without a nail, without any tools; one has to struggle to accomplish even the most basic. Terribly primitive and dispiriting to see how the time goes without any visible accomplishments. One runs around whole days to borrow the absolutely most necessary items. It's a tough battle, but I don't lose spirit and optimism.....

Wednesday, January 28, 1929. Snow melted in my socks and then froze. For two days I had terrible pains, could barely stagger along, dragged myself to work. Now it's okay. Nose got frostbitten, but not so badly.

The cold snap hangs on. Already eight days at minus 50 degrees. The farmers around here have cut out all outside work. I only work a couple of hours like a wild man in order to get warm. As soon as you begin to freeze you immediately have to get into the house. I froze the tip of my nose and part of my cheek and still the cold seemed bearable. If there's a wind, then any activity outside is impossible.

January End. This week it was bitter cold. Despite this I worked clearing. It's hard. But I still get warm hacking bush. Rest periods aren't possible. In a minute one begins to shiver and then, right away, you have to quickly flee inside the house. At home everything is frozen. Like crystal balls—potatoes, bread, even raisins. We hack at the meat with an axe, it splinters like glass.

At nights I freeze in the lower bunk. Hans, one level above, just below the roof, sweats. I've just got two blankets and they don't keep me warm. At work I wear less than I did in Germany—only I have five pairs of stockings on my feet, with mocassins pulled over them. You can't wear leather boots.

The cold seems to effect the kidneys and bladder. The

cold now effects us as the water did in fall. Life isn't exactly easy. Indescribably primitive. I'm living 80 percent from meat. For work, I only have the axe—everything else is lacking.

Inside the house, the dust and dirt is terrible. I've even got dust in my nose. One gradually comes to the state in which we found the other settlers, dirty and ragged. That can be altered. But today we appreciate what it means—to darn socks, to patch pants and underwear, the seams on the mocassins. Everything keeps coming apart. If you wanted to keep everything fixed there would hardly be time left to work.

February 5. Saturday Ralph Kless was here. Sunday, Fischer and Schreiber. Monday, Butterwick, a Canadian who wanted to talk me into getting horses. Today, Oscar the failed trapper. So there was variety enough.

Hans received a rejection from his Trude today. He is suffering from it.

In summer we thought of the long winter evenings and wondered how we would fill them, what we would do. But now there are no long winter evenings. At half past eight we're dead tired and go to sleep. Writing and mending gets put off day after day. Is it the food? Vitality is quite lacking. The unbelievable difference between outside and inside our small house, where the little tin airtight roars sucking in the air. It warms you but also makes you sleepy. We don't even read much, rarely have something to read.

I eat like a lord but it seems to lack nutritional substance. Pounds of roast (without fat or bacon), minced meat, boiled meat, bouillon and rolled oats. Only meat, bread and oats.

February 6. The cold period has broken, but it's not spring yet. It's alright for working. I work in the morning and stop around noon. A chinook blew the cold weather out.....

February End. In February I spent eight days hunting moose, missed one that went by at 10 meters. A neighbour shot three during that time.

March 1. Yesterday morning a Chinook raged around us. In one single day patches of prairie earth appeared from the knee-high snow. It's melting and melting and endless pools of water are everywhere. It's stupendous, how the snow is eaten by the warm wind. Even if it doesn't look like spring, one still feels that something's coming. The crows are appearing. They fly high and amasingly they almost bark here, instead of their krah-krah at home. The contrast between home and our new life could not be made clearer. I'm laying out my flower garden, even though planting is two months away.

March 7. Since three days it is winter again, although not so extremely cold. Quite a bit going on here. Neighbour Kless put two horses in our barn and he comes every day to feed them. Yesterday Butterwick was here again trying to sell us horses.

April 20. Three weeks ago I was in Sexsmith. A nice change—twice to the movie, to a dance—but I'm happy to be back on my farm. Didn't earn anything. Worked with a farmer and learned a good deal.....

On returning I found letters from Kriesel, Hilde, Menzel and Doris. How they moved me, when I thought I had put them behind me, is not to be described. I'm working like a wild man for several days clearing land. There is so monstrously much left to do to reach my goal—40 acres clear. I live happy and content at this work as never before. The $175 from Uncle Karl and mother have freed me from financial worries. I'm eating well and sometimes take a break from work. I am out of the biggest trouble.....

May 11. Well—it was a little too much work. Out at four in the morning and back to cook supper around nine at night. The wonderful, very early spring made it possible to break four more acres which, if all goes well, will be sown with oats by the middle of next week. *It's a good feeling to have four acres under the plow.* I wanted to be careful, it is already quite late and possibly it won't pay to seed.

Everything is growing in the garden as well—but will I be able to enjoy it? I will have to work out soon. Hans is still here; he's building in the fall.

(*Next entry*)...*July 16.* I have given up the battle. Thirty-two acres are all that I intend to clear. Nevertheless, that's a pretty good performance. Swinging the axe all day, always the same crazed rooting around. No more. Water shortage, no meat, no potatoes.

Eva has become engaged—it's all the same to me. It shows the absolute unreliability of women. Did I come to Canada because of this girl???

July 1929. Around the house the flowers are blooming. My garden, as small as it is, is good. Lots of salad greens, in fact the best cabbage in the Heart Valley. A pair of birds have established themselves in the house and the young birds give me much delight. Apart from that I'm dirty, live dirty and stupid.

1930

(Next diary entry)...January 4, 1930. How did the old year go out? It was cold outside and within myself as well; this cold—35 to 45 degrees below zero—uses up tremendous energy. One becomes every more stupified. Heat and the horrible mosquitoes in summer, in winter this cold. There are no great phrases, no chilling stories about how it freezes. But four weeks of minus 40 degrees celsius dull one more than a year of the hardest work.

I've made my house comfortable. Maybe it's one of the most cosy in Heart Valley. It doesn't help any. Everyone from home thinks of me and are concerned about me. What good is that? Kurt wrote a friendly letter. I'm getting on in harmony with Hans again. The same with all the neighbours, that one sees so seldom.

We had Christmas with Mr. and Mrs. Rosinski—one couldn't have celebrated it any better. Work goes forward slowly. Still what good is it? Now the hope is—a wife. Yah, about a wife and family—that's what we all dream of.....

Life here is a struggle against oneself. The smothering of all wishes. A good book, good music, culture is what is lacking in us and around us. This damned freedom, that one may be dirty. That one can get by without a collar, without any sort of refinement. All that I once experienced as narrowness, as personal restrictions—how gladly would I give up my so-called freedom to have some culture.

Sometimes I work on my farm, sometimes at Fischer's. I have nothing. It's not going yet. Next year maybe. And that's the thing—by the time you achieve your desires you will be already dreamed out.

Moose hunting and the other activities are necessities. "Necessity," a damned bitter word; it deadens and takes away the attractivenss of everything. Just now after Christmas, visiting is coming alive a bit. From now on I will see that I either have visitors or go visiting every Sunday. But that can be deadening too. Because visiting between us eight men can be even more dreary than being alone. Each has his own hopes, which he carries and nurtures and which sustain him. You know them, one and all. But it's the only thing that all have, that everybody talks about.

Sunday, January 5, 1930. Cooked the whole day, mended clothes but in reality everything is still in shreds. Sawed wood for an hour—minus 25 degrees celsius, so not too cold. But too cold to work. I don't have an inner body warmth anymore. Before noon I was in a part of the farm that I don't know well. Wanted to see what can be made of it. Wonders, in time, I imagine. Am now building a stool. This evening I wanted to go to Hans' to play chess.

(Instead of visiting Hans, Koeppen begins to look over photos of old friends in Germany. He is much moved by Eva's photo. Diary entry ends, "What devil is in that girl?)

January 6. In the morning a frightful cold. The thermometer doesn't register it anymore. It was at least 50 to 60 below zero in the morning, 24 degrees below at mid-day and minus 22 celsius in the evening, because the sky became clouded over. That's the Peace River. Tomorrow morning there could be a chinook or it could be miserably cold again. I believe the latter. What demands this makes on the body and on energy—at minus 30 degrees working is not describable.

Today I sawed wood and was horrified by the cooking—frozen, sweetish potatoes. It's impossible to keep potatoes unfrozen in the house. Then I cleared land. It's work that I always do with the old joy, where one can see the productive result. Reading a bit of *Conversations with Goethe* by Ackerman.(*comments on Truth and Meaning.*)

January 7. Today was a good day for working. Cleared land busily today. Up at 6:30, to work at 8:30, one and a half hours for lunch and quit at 6. To bed at the stroke of 9. Spent the evening cooking and reading. Today I lived in my thoughts, how I would spend evenings like this with my wife. If only I wouldn't spin these dreams out. There is always the danger that actualities will be disappointing.....

I can't get down to writing. The thoughts are there but something is missing. I can't complete anything whole, can't concentrate on anything. The thoughts wander in all regions and distances. Well then, nothing.

Wednesday. It got colder.

Friday, January 10. Today Fischer was here with horses and sled to help me. I have to work two days for it. Well, lumber for the chicken house is here. Fischer has many, not all exactly pleasant sides. Who doesn't have them? So of course like most of us, he believes always to act like a decent human being.

January 12. Herman Schreiber was here in the morning to ask about his money. It's terrible, but I don't have any. Bathed, washed clothes, cooked, did small jobs around the house. Tomorrow am going over to Fischer's to work for three to four days. How unwilling I am to go.

January 19. Worked three days at Fischer's. Miserably cold. Am reading Gottfried Keller, *Titus and Timotheus*...So, high up in the north, I sit in my small dirty log hut, minus 35 degrees outside, the airtight roars so that it glows. And I read and think possibly the very same things that someone else does in a fine dwelling in Berlin.

On Wednesday we frustratedly worked on a well at Fischer's in the almost unbearable cold. I froze part of my face, and Fischer his nose. At home everything was frozen. One really can't work in this weather but staying home eight days or longer is almost suicide.

January 25. Hans was here twice, worked another three days at Fischer's. He's drilled a 55 foot well, without success. Fischer, in his brutal manner, drove a horse to it's death. I am astounded about myself, how little I'm moved by the painful death of the horse. The animal died of a twisted intenstine. It was an ugly affair.

Yesterday Fischer was here. Firewood, fence posts, and logs to build with are ready.

January 27. What a time I have behind me. Last night—it was bitter cold. I crept out of bed, as I always do when it's cold, at about three in the morning and laid wood in the embers of the stove—a little tin one-hole heater that quickly roars and throws a lot of heat. Half awake, I hardly knew what I did. Then back to bed.

Around five o'clock I woke up coughing, head throbbing and almost drowned in smoke. Fire in the roof—that's to say the earth packed around the stove pipe glows and burns. Smoke, ash and glowing embers are falling into the room. I jump out of bed in my long underwear and try to get the fire out with the pail of water I have. Naturally the water wasn't enough but it helped, so that I could throw on some clothes. Then scratched out the earth around the stove pipe, and threw snow on the glowing embers, careful they were all out.

That would have made some film. But it turned out okay. No great damage and I'm alive. My dog was upset and he barked the whole time like crazy. He's not an especially bright hound but he's company anyway. He's losing his hair—a sort of mange—and I always carefully rub him with a mixture of lard and flower of sulphur that Michell gave me. It seems to help and it looks like the hair is growing back. But naturally he can't stand much cold.

January 28. Worked on the barn. In the evening Hans and Fischer were here. Nothing much; Fischer and I read and Hans went home. Made fence posts and nests for the chicken house. Tomorrow am going over to Fischer's, from there we are all going out to get logs. I'm restless. Need money, want to get ready. Wrote many letters.

February 2. Was at Fischer's this week. Cutting bush has become very difficult, although the weather is pleasant. The two feet of snow is now difficult to work in.

March 2. How the time goes. Was over at Guenther Licht's for three weeks. Have been home three days. I get along well with Licht. Now I'm working well. Guenther is coming over on Thursday to help me build.....

March 11. Guenther Licht is staying here and we're working to build a barn. Guenther is a complex person, stuffed with ideals and on the other hand still very self-centered. Does life here make us all like that? I like him a good deal.

The only fundamental thing right now—I believe more and more that Hilde Harang is the right wife for me. Would she want to? I don't feel fulfilled.

March 18. Guenther is still here. The weather has changed again and it's snowing. Two historic moments: 1) the first horse in the new barn; 2) the first pail of good tasting water.

(*The next entry*) *May 1930.* Well, in the meantime the pond ran dry. Worked at Herman Schreiber's eight days. It wasn't so nice. At Guenther's for a week. Then I got sick. Who knows what it is? Kidney pains. Maybe it stems from the water. I still have pain today. It was galling; not really sick but not capable of working. One could hang oneself from the frustration.

Mother sent me $50, which was a big help. The most important thing of the moment is *the letter* to Hilde.

(*The next entry*) *October 1, 1930.* Conditions have become unbearable. I've played myself out, am worn out. Life like this is horrible. Living like this, without a wife, is slow suicide. Slow spiritual death. Even my love of animals and gardening doesn't move me anymore. All of us here have reached the zero point.....

Even financial success is out. The harvest was staggering here. But the price—oats, 15 cents a bushel—a catastrophe. I'm looking at a quite terrible winter ahead. Barely enough to live on. And that after my heart was filled with joy and pride last summer as I looked out over the fields. Such a wonderful picture of well-being. The blue-green oats stood like a wall, it grew and grew. The leaves so broad. So many stalks from the same kernel, and then how they filled out. Big, full, juicy grains.

And now, not a step ahead and an absolute spiritual deadening. A slow degeneration in dirt and routine. An actual animalization. I live like an animal, only the most necessary natural drive, sexual satisfaction, isn't possible.

Koeppen's first Peace River homestead cabin, Heart Valley, 1929

Trekking south from the Peace River, Ebe and Hilde, 1937.

So I stand below the animals. The crucial role that the other sex plays in the whole level of life only we here can truly appreciate.

Why are we here, without hope? Why do we vegetate here without any future? I don't know. Go back?—that's closed off for three years, until I can sell off. Building up was my answser, the only one I had. But what for? Not even for others. Sometime later the farm will all rot away and fall apart. If one marries, you need a wonderful wife for this life. Everyone here eats, drinks, and goes about their work, but all in deadly dullness.

October 23, 1930. (Koeppen has now acquired some livestock; pigs, two cows and calves, and assorted poultry. His optimism has returned, as well as a philosophizing bent on Eva, love and so forth.)

1931

(Next entry) June 15, 1931. Ja—God knows, still in Canada on my homestead. Worked, got ahead a little. Had some happy hours by myself or working with the livestock. Apart from that this life is growing impossible. I have to hold on for two years more now in any case. What I wrote about Eva months ago is today still true. That's understandable. When I think that in all the years in Canada I've gotten to very briefly meet four to six girls. All attempts at marriage wreck anyway on the catastrophic state of the economy. I would not have previously believed such a collapse in prices was possible.

The only development: another complete break with Hans. In general, a break with the increasingly morbid dependence on this small circle of people. Desire for theatre, opera, cafe, tie and collar, culture. Increasing interest in gardening. The acquisition of my fabulous saddle horse, Baby.

I will try to systematically record my activities for some days.

Today, forenoon, took care of livestock. Now have one horse, and what an unimaginable help that is. Also have chickens, geese, turkeys, one sow, two cows with calves and six steers that are out to pasture.

Afternoon, filled water in whatever containers I have. I'm still farming without water. A situation that makes your hair stand on end. The last three days we had a heavy rain that filled some hollows. Afterwards hoed potatoes until the evening. Right hard, since it is new land. Planted some beets. Supper. And now a wonderful evening task—an hour going up and down hill (sometimes two hours) searching for the cows. Some better solution must be found. There are too many daily minor chores that have to be done. The days are really long. It's light as day till eleven o'clock.

June 16. Well, it's like this. In the morning, I was still in bed. Fischer comes along looking for his horses that have broken out. Our fences are only so-so. A little barbed wire hung here and there. Often from tree to tree. And at the valley end the animals can just walk out. Which they always seem to do.

As I came to the barn I found that the cows had destroyed the feedbox. Naturally they had scattered large amounts of oats all over. So I had to use the forenoon repairing the grainery.

About noon old Kless popped up—as always he wanted something. This time I gave up some beet plants. A few minutes later Schreiber came along, naturally for lunch. Well, he can't help it and I'm glad to have guests. I sold him a turkey.

In the afternoon I had to fix up the pig pen. In the evening, planting beets. Continually in motion but without results. Yesterday evening I had the pleasure of wading through the Bad-Heart three times to get the cows. Couldn't get hold of Baby. I fail to understand why these beasts have to cross that stream. Since the rains there is about two and a half feet of rushing water in it. Oh, did I curse.

June 17. Hoed potatoes in forenoon. They look pretty good but before they're harvested and in nobody knows what will happen. From mid-August on the daily hope begins that there'll be no frost, and sometimes it can even freeze in July. Around noon I noticed that the horses had made themselves scarce. It's like to drive you mad. I first went through the meadow by the valley, then over to Scriba's. Without success. Then it started to rain again very steadily. I couldn't go to the post office because of the horses. Am waiting for a letter from Kurt. I recently got a sign of life from him—a post card.

Art Noreen just came and told me that the horses and foals and the little moose are all on the other side of the Bad-Heart. So, got to go.

June 18. (More on chasing cows across the Bad-Heart, and waiting for letters.)

The situation with Hans is almost laughable, that such petty things can drive people apart. I owed him five dollars for green feed, which I'll naturally give him when I have money. As I rode across his place my sow followed me, without my knowing it. She's in heat. Besides, she doesn't like to stay alone and often follows me all over the farm, followed by the three geese at a respectful distance. So anyway, Hans got hold of her and corralled her and immediately demanded payment for the green feed. It put me off so much that the friendship is disolved. It's so stupid.

June 19. (Long entry on trying to round up a cow that is supposed to be taken to a neighbour's to be bred. Without success.)

June 20. Working out at Schuster's in morning. Working on dugout in afternoon. Searching for cows in the evening.

June 21. Up at 6:30 and over to Foster's where I chop stumps. Around 5 in the evening I had the pleasure to observe, at a distance on the other side of the Bad-Heart, how my cows slowly made their way around the fences and drew off in the direction of freedom, disappearing in the bush. Ah, what a joy! To my great astonishment I found them peacefully grazing on a meadow on our side of the Bad-Heart on my way home. Incredible.

June 22. Up early, at 6 o'clock over to Michell's where I will work two days for a turkey and two pounds of butter.

June 23. Out early at 5 o'clock. First had to look for the horses one and a half hours. As I was just scrabbling to the top of the other side of the valley I saw them, standing a short distance from the barn. Scriba picked up his foal, which was ill. At Michell's clearing land. Drove in cows at night and didn't get to bed till 10:30.

June 24. Had to search half an hour for horses again; then to Scriba's. Working at Scriba's with Fischer making barbed wire fences slung from tree to posts. At night over to Michell's, who picked up my post. Saved me four miles. A letter from Hilde.

June 25. Baking bread. Well, not real bread. More like bachelor's biscuits. Don't have an oven. But a good lunch—spinach, omellete, potatoes, salad and thickened milk. Every day I eat two bowls of thickened milk. Letters from Kriessel, Mother, and Hilde. Will anything ever develop with Hilde? I don't think so. Licht didn't come over, as he said he would. Have to go over to Scriba's to help another day tomorrow.

June 26. Over to Scriba's in the morning and spent the whole day digging out the well. It's a heavy compact clay, that one has to wearily break out in little pieces. No water in the "well", it just fills with melt water in the spring.

July 1, 1931. Gathering roots. That is to say, hacked, and grubbed, and wrestled them out. The most miserable work there is. Otto brought me some boards. Some fifteen miles away where the Seventh-Day Adventists live there is a sawmill that operates in the winter. A letter to Aunt Kathe and Hilde. Thoughts and stimulation hardly exist in this kind of life. At noon I read a little from the *Free Press Prairie Farmer* and sometimes from a novel. I have hardly any difficulties in reading English now. Now to get the cows.

1932

(Next entry) January 15, 1932. The maddest northwest storm I have ever experienced is raging outside. Even beside the stove I'm freezing. Apart from that, this winter has been quite without severe cold.

Actually I should close off this diary completely since the periods between the entries are too long. A few days ago I read the diaries through from beginning to end. I ended the first two books only with great effort, such drawn-out, boring twaddle.....

It appears that I've always reached for the diary when I was in a bad mood. There are some quite frightful things in it about the first winter. There is nothing in the diary of the many joys.....

I am determined to be a real farmer with animals, garden and all that goes with it, instead of just breaking land in order to plant grain. Have planted not only flowers and garden but also bush fruit that's native to the country. The best are Saskatoons, big, fat blue berries that often weigh down the bush. And there are choke cherries, sharp and sour, but make good wine. Everything grows well, but the frost often comes and destroys it. The water question is unfortunately only partly solved. In the summer the animals drink down by the Bad-Heart and I use the water in the dugout that every spring is filled by the melting snow. It's not exactly good. In the winter we melt snow and ice. If we cover it with straw it lasts a long time. Our straw piles are invaluable. The threshing machine blows the straw into big heaps and horses and cows stand around them even in 50 below zero weather, eating and out of the wind. Soon the straw stacks look like giant mushrooms. The pigs dig themselves deep into the trampled-down straw and on cold days only pop up briefly to eat and then quickly disappear again.

The next neighbour is Hans who is about a mile away, then comes Scriba, about two miles. But I can't see their houses since the woods are in between. But far away, over the Bad-Heart, is Foster's house. And on real cold days I can see the smoke from their house rising. But in winter it's almost impossible to ride there.....

(*Long passages on how much he has changed since leaving Germany, on how distant he is from old relationships. At the same time the diary rakes over old contentions with these same people. Extended comments on how much better off he is on the Peace River homestead and how contented he is. A final passage indicates an incipient case of being "bushed".*)

...I am becoming completely sufficient unto myself—enjoy all letters, enjoy every visit, but don't really need them. I am busy and feel well. It is the right work for me. No radio or music and yet my little hut is comfortable. Certain occurences here are not pleasant. The less one needs others the more peacefully and happily one can live.....

January 18. Yesterday I rode bareback to Wanham. That's eighteen miles, thirty-six miles there and back. The railway station is in Wanham. Also a store, a blacksmith and a hotel. Our city! Oh, I almost forgot, there's a small restaurant as well. They even have movies once a week in winter, but naturally it's too far to ride for that.

We have to team the grain there, once we get on our feet and have a sleigh. Right now Scriba delivers my grain. I get one-third of the harvest that reaches the elevator. There are two of them on the rail line. When it's cold or storms, it's often a long, terrible trip by sleigh. *Last fall* I had a lot of pain and a hard time because of my miserable sciatica. Wrapped my leg in a cat's pelt but it helped only a bit. I would get up at 5:30 to look after the stock and then ten hours of road work. Partly to work off taxes and partly for some cash. I would feed the stock at night and cook for the next day. And always this miserable pain. That went on for four weeks. I had no idea of what was wrong and what might develop if that would continue. Finally I had forty dollars and quit. Getting ill or injured is naturally a terrible thought, especially since often you don't see anyone for days. In the winter time, now, it could have tragic consequences. I often think that what is needed most are not even good roads, but telephones. But those are a long, long way off. Our roads—trails— are often impassable. They are like soap in the spring, after every rain. The heavy clay earth becomes a rubbery mud and makes everything slippery. And in winter you're often snowed in.

(Next entry) March 14, 1932. Yesterday I tried to ride to the post office since I haven't been "out" for two weeks. But I had to turn in at Fischer's and stop. Baby was completely played out going through the chest-high snow. It blows like fine sand and in a moment the tracks are covered again. Fischer got to the post office once by sled. He wants to try to get a load of grain to the main road tomorrow, which is in better condition. And then take it to Wanham the day after. He has to break a path four miles to the main road.

I've got enough fodder for the animals, enough for myself, and also enough firewood—so it's not absolutely necessary that I get out. But bit by bit I'm yearning to know if the remaining world still exists.....

March 18. The sow gave birth to eighteen piglets, all frozen rockhard, and the worst is that I feel guilty about it. I had moved her over into the barn, which I thought was better and warmer since the two horses, three cows and poultry are in there. But through moving her over she became restless and apparently did not bed herself down well enough for the piglets. I expect the cow to calve in a few days; hopefully all will go well.

March 19. We had a chinook and already patches of black earth are appearing. It is an unpleasant, raw, cool wind but still it gobbles up the snow. The oldtimers here have never seen so much snow here.

Of course, there are no real oldtimers here. The first came only about ten years ago to this district, mostly veterans from the World War who arrived about 1918 or 1920 or so. They are good people but we don't see enough of each other to really become friends. And I still have some difficulties with the language. Most are married and have children. I should have mentioned that we all got together for a Christmas concert in the one room school. Everybody had to do his little piece.

March 20. The chinook is still blowing—one only sees ice here and there now. The wind is quite cool and unpleasant. I still have much to learn to be a farmer here.

March 28. The black earth steams in the sun and it tempts me to prepare the fields. But ten centimeters down it is still frozen.

March 30. I'M ENGAGED'. In Hilde I've got a girl who really is suited to Canada. I love her. Her personality harmonizes well with mine. I worry a little about her clear, self-confident manner. If she believes she knows something then that's the way it is. That's how they all are. She's a little young for our life here. She's only 22. But during the last few years she's had a sad and ordered life with her aunts. I think her heart has longed for love and youth, that she matured quickly under that pressure. I believe that women mature earlier and are more practical than men anyway. Now I yearn and hope. Heart and spirit filled with love and tenderness. In short, quite in the condition of a bridegroom. (*Etc., etc.*) Will it work out? I'm hoping, although I foresee many difficulties.

April 5. I'm working on a new log house. In the evenings I'm building a cabinet.

May 9. Busily building a yard fence out of small tree trunks. To make a large corral for the calves and pigs. During the day I work on the fences. The pasture is quite large and I always feed some oats so the horses come back. I keep the two calves at home and when the milk "presses" the cows come home. The pasture is still pretty thin. It only began to get green in the beginning of May.

May 14. Sowing is getting into full swing. My dugout is full of water, melted snow that ran off the fields. The house is becoming quite comfortable.....

May 17. The day is set. Hilde will arrive here July 26. There are still a thousand things to complete. It must really be difficult for her, to set off into a strange world, when she hasn't seen me in four years.....

Uncle Karl sent me the $250 that I have to deposit (*with Canadian Immigration*) and only get back after the marriage. What would we have done without that.

May 22. Dug like a wild man. The clay is like cement and the work progresses frightfully slowly. Fischer is to bring me stumping powder, so I can blast. Got a bit softer after I got through the frost but not easier—now it's like rubber. I'm nine feet down now and it's progressively more difficult to get the earth out. When Hilde's here it'll be easier because then she can raise the buckets.

May 25. It worked; blew out all four feet clean. But now it's rock hard and I can't go any further. No water. The livestock drink down on the Bad-Heart and the pigs still have two feet of water in the slough. Will dig a water hole beside that and hope that the water which collects will be without mosquitoes.

May 31. The geese have laid and are brooding. The turkeys have disappeared although they pop up from time to time. Do the coyotes get them? There are many field mice that the coyotes busily hunt and a lot of rabbits this year as well.....

Thank God that this year we have fewer mosquitoes. Usually I only make a smudge fire in the evenings. Smoke with manure and grass—that keeps the blood-thirsty beasts away. We now have mosquitoe netting on the windows.

June 4. The days fly, hardly time to dream.....

June 7. At the moment we have cold nights. Frost danger.

June 9. How will I complete everything? I do what I can, but I need a few hours sleep too. We need rain. The grain has come up well. We're doing some seeding still.

July 4. The neighbours are helping me finish last things on house. Mrs. Rosinsky is really a fabulous cook. I wonder if Hilde can cook? My bachelor cooking is rather plain, even if it's all from good fresh food. She will hardly miss electricity now. It's still daylight now when we go to bed. But in winter, with the coal oil lamps that never give enough light and often stink—?

We're all excited. Dog, cat, horse and me. Only the cows don't notice anything and the pigs couldn't care less. I've bought a real good stove and some other things, on credit, even the ring. Have borrowed a suit for the wedding that may be a bit large but should do. Our new log house with the big windows and the bought door is quite pretty. Even tacked up a big towel embroidered with windmills as a background to the stove. The paint I made from powder, oil and salt turned out quite well. All the visitors wonder at the dumbwaiter from the cellar. I got it out of a book distributed by the government. Apart from that I designed and built everything myself with the help of the neighbours.

The steamer trunk looks okay and serves as a washstand. The sofa, which is actually only a box upholstered with straw sacks, is a bit hard but will do. There are enough windows so that it's bright and friendly—not like the first shack. All that's lacking are some trees and hedges around the house. On the other hand, the view is that much better without them. Only in winter the wind will blow awfully cold. If we only had water, good and in quantity.

140

July 9, 1932. Yesterday Scriba said to me, "Well, if you don't hit it off, there are lots of others looking for a wife around here." Oh, it has to work. Hilde must be underway already

July 12, 1932. Fischer says that everyone wants to meet the train and welcome the bride. That worries me. After the long trip, tired and exhausted, not knowing the languge and not having seen me for four years, that will be too much.

I'm going to meet the train at the station before Wanham. Hilde and I have to go to Spirit River in order to make our marriage declarations in front of the Justice of the Peace anyway. Fischer can meet the preacher in Wanham. Marriages are truly an extraordinary event here.....

July 25, 1932. I can hardly work. Sit and plan and hope. Hope that everything goes well. That Hilde will be contented and happy here. There will always be enough to live on and maybe next year we will be able to afford a radio. I hope she has as much joy from the animals as I. I run here and I run there and hardly know what I'm doing.

Bibliography
A Handful of Reading

There exists a vast and still growing mass of books on homesteading in the Canadian West. While many are to some extent imbued with the Horatio Alger pioneer myth most also entail accounts of value and accuracy. The handful of books mentioned here are not necessarily the most definitive ones and are merely my personal suggestions for further reading.

Some context of Arnt Arntzen's experiences in pre-W.W. I United States can be gotten from Kenneth Allsop's *Hard Travelin'* (1967). Something of the work, living conditions and struggles of the railway workers during the "great boom" in B.C. appears in Jack Scott's *Plunderbund and Proletariat* (1975). Accounts of farming and ranching on the Canadian prairies from the 1920's, through the great depression and to the 1940's are extremely numerous and one can only arbitrarily suggest Seymour Lipsett's *Agrarian Socialism* (1959), relevant sections of Barry Broadfoot's *Ten Lost Years* (1973), despite its strenuous attempts to exclude political views, and Jean Burnet's *Next Year Country* (1951).

Wallace Stegner's *Wolf Willow* (1955) is a reminiscence of suitcase farming during the World War I period in the Cypress Hills dry belt, a region to the southeast of where Koeppen began his work in Canada as a farm hand. While Stegner's fictionalized history of the region is too fictional, his personal reminiscences of that time and especially his reflections on what often happens to such communities a generation or so after settlement are insightful, provocative and moving.

For the Peace River homesteading we have C.A. Dawson and R.W. Murchie's *The Settlement of the Peace River District, a study of a pioneer area* (1934). It is a volume in a series on Canadian Frontiers of Settlement which in the late

1920's and 1930's brought together work of historians, geographers, economists and rural sociologists. It is especially valuable since it was done during the very period when Koeppen was keeping his diary. While the Peace River Settlement study is somewhat stilted and tinged with the bias of its time, it is a valuable scholarly overview. *Peace River Chronicles* (1963), edited by Gordon Bowes, provides a balance to the above University of Toronto study. It relies mainly on accounts written by those who lived and worked in that area during the time; homesteaders and others. Many of these accounts are vibrant and alive, even if sometimes baudlerized and somewhat given to the "old time pioneer" orientation. About a half of the book deals with the homesteading phases of the region.

The Great Depression in the cities and non-farming areas of Western Canada has become documented by an increasing number of scholarly and personal accounts. Some experience of conditions in Vancouver and other parts of B.C. during that time can be obtained from Ronald Liversedge's *Recollections of the On-To-Ottawa Trek* (1960), Rolf Knight's *A Very Ordinary Life* (1974) and from more external (possibly more comprehensive) histories such as Martin Robin's *The Rush for Spoils* (1972) and *Pillars of Profit* (1974).

Sidney Hutcheson's *Depression Stories* (1977) is a personal narrative of many lives and events in the Kootenays during that decade. Although Hutcheson was not a stump rancher himself his stories are set in a region where that kind of rural settlement was inextricably linked with regional conditions. To my knowledge no easily available account exists which in depth details stump ranch life, although it is broached by many local histories and more personal tales. Possibly Lester Peterson's *The Cape Scott Story* (1974), dealing with an atypically isolated area of aspirant but failing homesteads, is the closest we have to such a history. While numerous books and coffee table documentaries on the life of loggers and other primary resource workers have recently appeared, as yet there is no truly reliable and rounded account of camp life in B.C. during this period. Issues of the journal *Raincoast Chronicles* (1973-) (especially issues 3 to 5 dealing with logging and fishing in B.C.) provide as much feel for these worlds as anything else.

To my knowledge there is also no generally available book on communal farms and settlements in B.C. One may turn to an account of earlier communal settlements in a nearby region, Charles LeWarne's *Utopias On Puget Sound, 1885-1915* (1975). A very brief pop-journalistic treatment is "The Edens of Erewhon" in Steward Holbrook's *Far Corner* (1952). The collected papers and writings of Watson Thomson (the man who founded the Serpentine Valley communal farm) are held by the University of British Columbia and may be of interest to students.

Finally, there are libraries of reminiscences of events similar to those discussed in the present narrative in the memories of many men and women who experienced them. They can be a powerful vehicle in transmitting history.